SONOMA VALLEY STYLE

AT HOME IN CALIFORNIA'S WINE COUNTRY

SONOMA VALLEY STYLE

AT HOME IN CALIFORNIA'S WINE COUNTRY

Kathryn Masson

Photography by Steven Brooke

RIZZOLI
NEW YORK

For James Beauchamp Alexander,
Suzanne Brangham, and David Pashley
　　　　—Kathryn Masson

For Suzanne and Miles
　　　　—Steven Brooke

Front cover: Tuscan Country House (p. 92)
Back cover: Hispano Moorish Residence (p. 150)

Page 1: Mediterranean-California Ranch (p. 80)

Previous pages: MacArthur Place, located four
blocks from Sonoma Plaza on what was once
a 300-acre vineyard and working horse and cattle
ranch, is now a top-rated hotel and spa in the
Zagat Survey. Its seven acres of spectacular gardens
complement the Victorian-inspired 64-guest-room
complex that includes a restored circa 1860
farmhouse, new guest cottages, a day spa, and
a restaurant.

Right: The main guest house and guest cottages
of MacArthur Place, Sonoma Valley's premier
boutique inn and spa, are built in a charming
Victorian style. Numerous landscaped courtyards
throughout the complex create an intimate,
luxurious atmosphere.

First published in the United States of America in
2005 by
Rizzoli International Publications, Inc.
300 Park Avenue South, New York, NY 10010
www.rizzoliusa.com

ISBN: 0-8478-2720-8
LCCN: 2004116264
© 2005 Rizzoli International Publications, Inc.
Photographs © 2005 Steven Brooke
Text © 2005 Kathryn Masson

Designed by Abigail Sturges

Printed and bound in China

2005 2006 2007 2008 2009 / 10 9 8 7 6 5 4 3 2 1

CONTENTS

INTRODUCTION

The lure of the Sonoma Valley for twenty-first-century travelers and its fortunate residents lies in the balance of its rural environment from which some of the world's most sophisticated agricultural products originate, its picturesque rusticity, and its cosmopolitan culture. One of the many charms of the Sonoma Valley is that it captures much of California's colorful history through fine examples of the state's architectural development. These styles include original Mexican-period adobes, nineteenth-century Victorian farmhouses, restored early-twentieth-century Craftsman bungalows, remodels of modern "California" ranch houses, and contemporary residences on the cutting edge of the design world today. As architectural historian James Beauchamp Alexander aptly explains in his seminal work *Sonoma Valley Legacy*, "It is this representative collection of historic houses which revives the feeling of continuity so totally lacking in so many of California's newer communities." This is the essence of the irreplaceable timeless quality and charm of the Sonoma Valley.

Much of the early culture and history of Northern California centers around events that began in 1824 in the area that later became Sonoma County, particularly in the town of Sonoma in the Sonoma Valley, then under Mexican rule. The only lasting role of the final pre-Europeans to reside in the valley, mainly the Pomo,

Previous pages: Founded in 1973, Chateau St. Jean Vineyards and Winery, a consistent producer of top award-winning wines, is one of the Sonoma Valley's most picturesque winetasting settings. Located at the foot of Sugarloaf Ridge in Kenwood, its formal gardens, elegant tasting room, and terrace overlooking the rolling green lawn are favorite spots for special events.

Right: A landscape of rolling hills dotted with oak trees identifies the Sonoma Valley as the quintessential terrain of early California history. Today conservation-aware residents, vintners, and farmers protect this open countryside whose ambiance defines the region.

Coastal Miwok, and Miyakamas tribes, was to attract missionaries. The Native American population waned after a small-pox epidemic in 1836, and they were essentially gone by the 1880s, leaving behind a legacy of place names. Their demise brought an end to the era of adobe construction. The influence of the first Old World settlement in what would become Sonoma County did not last.

This was Fort Ross, established in 1812 by Russian fur traders on the Pacific coastline eighty-five miles north of San Francisco to serve as a foothold for Russia in inter-national colonization. That settlement was held in check by the Mexican government and Fort Ross was eventually purchased by Captain John Sutter in 1840, never becoming more than an obscure outpost. A confluence of personalities, conditions,

and events brought the Sonoma Valley its prominent role in California history. Padre Jose Altimira and later Comandante-Generale Mariano Guadalupe Vallejo played decisive roles in these events. The founding of the town was based more on these men's religious and political objectives than on economically determined geographical choices. It was Altimira who established the site for the mission in 1824. Then in 1835

Mission San Francisco de Solano, the last of California's missions, was originally built on the edge of the Sonoma Plaza in 1824. It has been rebuilt through the years, and is now a sturdy adobe structure. Rooms adjacent to the chapel house special exhibitions and an orientation office open to the public.

was followed by the United States seizing control of California in 1848. With the discovery of gold shortly thereafter, the business and population of California changed forever. Personal economics replaced empire-building as new communities were formed. More than any other town in the state, Sonoma bridged the gap between the Mexican colonial past and California's future.

Spanish colonization of coastal California was accomplished through the establishment of four Royal Presidios and a string of missions from San Diego to San Francisco. It is ironic that the twenty-first and final "Spanish" mission, in Sonoma, was founded after Mexico's 1822 independence from Spain. Padre Jose Altimira, a Spaniard who had refused to sign a loyalty oath to Mexico, led an expedition from Mission Dolores in Yerba Buena to the outlying countryside to found a more northern, inland mission where ailing neophytes living on the chilly, damp peninsula might live in a healthier, sunnier climate. In 1824 this anachronistic idealist established Mission San Francisco de Solano in what would become the town of Sonoma. Originally built of redwood, the church was rebuilt in adobe in 1829.

In August 1834, the Mexican Republican Congress ordered secularization of all of the Spanish missions in California and the division of their lands. The Sonoma

Vallejo was assigned to use the area as a base for military operations and Mexican colonization. The town of Sonoma was situated on Sonoma Creek, miles above any point reachable by ship. Though there was a landing at the mouth of Sonoma Creek near the bay, the town was never a major commercial center. The Sonoma Valley was blessed by a temperate climate, sustaining fresh water, estuaries to the south that yielded plentiful seafood, and rolling hills of grassland, savanna, and forest that provided abundant wildlife and rich soils. These factors did little more than make it convenient for Altimira and later Vallejo to pursue their goals. Sonoma was the last major California town established under colonial assumptions, forces that had driven the settlement of California's older pueblos. Mexican independence from Spain

congregation dwindled and the original church building collapsed. Although other church buildings were built and destroyed, the restored adobe parish church built by General Vallejo in 1840–41 still stands. Of the original mission complex, portions of the padres' living quarters that adjoined the parish church and two rooms thought to be a part of the majordomo's residence have been incorporated into later construction. Today, the Blue Wing Hotel, built in 1849 and still standing on Spain Street across from the mission, is thought to contain the two rooms of the majordomo's quarters.

In 1835, Mariano Guadalupe Vallejo, the ambitious twenty-four-year-old Comandante of the Presidio in San Francisco, was appointed by his friend Jose Figueroa, Governor of Alta California, to establish a military presence in nearby Sonoma, administer the secularization of the mission, and distribute the mission's lands. As commander of the military forces in Northern California, Vallejo built the Sonoma Barracks as a military stronghold to inhibit Russian expansion southward from Fort Ross. Vallejo was also charged with laying out a city. With a plaza as its center, the small town of Sonoma became well known throughout California for its social and political events. In return for his services, Vallejo was granted Rancho Petaluma, which eventually encompassed 66,000 acres. Its lands supported successful

Originally built in 1849 as the Sonoma House, the Blue Wing Hotel is California's oldest hostelry. It still stands today on Spain Street across from the mission, its adobe bricks revealed through layers of worn plaster, awaiting restoration. Once the most popular hotel and saloon in town, it housed such visitors as Lt. William Sherman and Charles Stone, who would later become famous during the Civil War.

cattle and sheep industries, crop production, and expansive vineyards whose vines had been uprooted from the mission's vineyards after secularization. With a passion for viticulture unequalled by any of his other interests, Vallejo managed these vineyards and eventually produced wines that won awards in statewide exhibitions. Additional large tracts of land were granted to his friends, aides, and family. Vallejo was in the forefront of the military, political, and social scenes in Sonoma, and in subsequent years, when his holdings grew to nearly 800,000 acres, he was said to be the richest man in California.

Vallejo encouraged Mexican citizens to settle in Northern California, but as time passed, Americans who had married his daughters and other relatives became his friends. His sympathy and admiration for Americans grew, despite living in an era of great distrust and hostility between the two nations. By the mid-1840s many Americans had immigrated to California. In 1846 a handful of disgruntled and angry Americans living in the Sonoma and Napa valleys staged the Bear Flag Revolt, claiming California independent of Mexican rule, and arresting and impris- oning General Vallejo. Unbeknownst to them, his sympathies had fallen with the

United States because he was disappointed with Mexico for its failure to fulfill its promises to support Sonoma. Although the revolt failed, Vallejo eventually spanned the gap between eras by assisting in the transition to American rule. As a sign that he supported the Americanization of the territory, his new home, named Lachryma Montis, which he built not far from the mission, was a Victorian style, prefabricated kit house.

Like other Northern California towns, Sonoma grew rapidly with the discovery of gold not far to the east (January 1848), possession of California by the United States (1848), and California statehood (September 1850). In the ensuing decades, land disputes, legal battles, and dishonest men stripped General Vallejo of his vast property. He never lost his personal integrity or his goodwill toward Sonoma, but by the time of his death in 1890 his only holdings were Lachryma Montis and twenty surrounding acres. At his funeral he was honored for his creation of Sonoma. Sonoma growth included adventurers lured by the gold fields, but also many others who bought or squatted on land where they raised horses, cattle, sheep, fruit trees, and grapes. Among these early settlers were Germans and Italians who had fled political upheaval and military pressure in their homelands. In the four succeeding decades, some of Sonoma's most famous wineries were started by European wine-making families with names such as Gundlach, Dresel, Bundschu, Simi, Quitzow, Foppiano, Korbel, and Sebastiani.

Simple wine production began to grow into an industry when Hungarian expatriate Agoston Haraszthy moved to Sonoma in search of perfect viticultural conditions. In 1857 he purchased a 570-acre estate in Sonoma from General Vallejo's brother Salvador, and named it Buena Vista. His energy, industry, and belief in Sonoma's potential as a world leader in the wine industry were unprecedented. During an extended trip to Europe, he shipped to California over 100,000 cuttings from more than 300 varieties of grapevines as well as the finest examples of olive, pomegranate, and citrus trees. Haraszthy later sold the varietals to farmers throughout California, quickly diversifying the types of wine produced in the state. He also published the results of experiments in grape growing and wine making in his *Report on Grapes and*

Left: The Sonoma Plaza, laid out as a quadrangle by General Mariano Guadalupe Vallejo to be the center of town, still serves that purpose. Specialty shops, restaurants, and a theater fill the spaces in the historic and new buildings that surround the plaza, a large public park where City Hall and the visitor informa-tion center are located.

Following pages: General Vallejo's neighbor and friend Agoston Haraszthy estab-lished Buena Vista Winery in 1857. Today, a 1989 repro-duction of the Pompeiian-style villa that Haraszthy built and gave to his son Atilla as a wedding present when he mar-ried Vallejo's daughter stands in the Bartholomew Memorial Park, part of Bartholomew Winery, which had been created from portions of Buena Vista Winery in the twentieth century.

Wine in California. His intention was to disseminate this information to all viticulturalists and vintners so that California's wine industry would succeed. He is called the "Father of Modern California Viticulture" primarily because of his determination to develop the state's wine industry into the best in the world.

Early in the history of wine making in Sonoma Valley, the phylloxera louse, which infects roots and completely destroys the grape vine, had been a threat. A phylloxera epidemic that began in 1869 destroyed virtually all of the vineyards in Sonoma by the late 1870s. By the mid 1870s, however, Julius Dresel, who was part-owner of Gundlach Bundschu (established c. 1858), one of the oldest wineries in Sonoma, solved the phylloxera problem by proving that rootstocks from plants indigenous to the Mississippi River Valley were phylloxera-resistant. He broke the destructive cycle of infestation by grafting European varietal vines onto the phylloxera-resistant roots. Sonoma's vineyards were replanted and thrived. In 1893 Sonoma and other California vintners displayed 301 varieties of wine at the Chicago World's Fair, and in 1900, while other Sonoma wines took medals at the Paris Exposition, Gundlach Bundschu took the gold.

The 1906 earthquake in San Francisco had devastating repercussions for the Sonoma wine industry. Wine caves in the valley crumbled and Sonoma wineries whose business and storehouse buildings were located in the downtown financial district of San Francisco burned down, destroying entire inventories of wine and all business records. The wine industry's mettle was again tried and again found to be strong. Winery businesses were eventually rebuilt. At the height of production in the early twentieth century, before the Volstead Act became law, there were 256 wineries, large and small, and more than 22,000 acres planted to vineyards in Sonoma County.

Prohibition, which lasted from 1919 to 1933, caused almost all of the wineries to close. A few remained active by making sacramental wine or producing grapes for grape juice. Vineyards, on the other hand, persisted. The law allowed that 200 gallons of wine could be made by each head-of-household in America per year for personal use. By Prohibition's end in 1933 there were still 21,000 acres of vineyards in production, and in the coming years wineries made a gradual comeback. Over several decades, Sonoma gradually reclaimed its history, though it was not until the nation's interest in wine boomed during the 1960s that Sonoma's wine industry took its great leap forward. Industry improvements, such as stricter labeling and identifying appellations, aided in this surge. Between 1960 and 2000 the number of Sonoma's wineries grew from 58 to 192, with nearly 58,000 acres planted to vineyards. Grapes are not only an integral part of Sonoma Valley's history, they are the county's most valuable agricultural product, accounting for almost eighty percent of its gross agricultural income.

In 2000 Sonoma County was the number one grape-growing region in California, and with related tourism, viticulture contributed $3 billion to the local economy. A considerable diversity is still represented in Sonoma's products, with businesses whose roots reach back to the nineteenth century. Today, dairy and poultry farms, cattle ranches, the largest equine industry in America, strawberry, cherry, apple, peach, citrus, nut, and honey businesses, and cheese and olive production,

prove that Sonoma County is truly one of America's most beautiful and thriving agricultural regions.

One of Sonoma's most picturesque wineries is Cline Cellars, established in 1991 on historic property located in the lower Sonoma Valley. Once the site of a Miwok village built around warm springs that still flow, the winery complex includes a refurbished circa 1858 farmhouse, one of Sonoma's earliest.

In the 1990s Sonomans approved a tax to generate revenue to purchase development rights of land threatened by urban sprawl. They have gone further to protect their agricultural setting by voting to create growth boundaries for major towns. Residents also recognize the importance of preserving their historically significant structures. Treasured nineteenth-century Victorian buildings have been refurbished and transformed into viable commercial properties. Others, like the carriage house at MacArthur Place, have been built to complement nearby restored nineteenth-century properties.

The popularity of nineteenth-century resorts such as Boyes Hot Springs and Fetters Hot Springs, immediately north of the Sonoma Plaza, is evidenced today in the abundance of bed-and-breakfasts, hotels, and spa/resorts that serve Sonoma visitors. The small mid-valley town of Glen Ellen has an inspiring wooded setting. Literary luminaries M.F.K. Fisher and Jack London made their homes there. Still-rural Kenwood, at the terminus of the Sonoma Valley proper, enjoys a serene location at the base of Sugarloaf Ridge. Kenwood's Chateau St. Jean Winery offers a glimpse of Old World European elegance in its tasting

Left: Cline Cellars, established in 1991 on historic property in the lower Sonoma Valley off Arnold Drive, features a circa 1858 farm-house as its tasting room. The winery's grounds, once the site of a Miwok settlement and the original site chosen for Mission de Solano (though a permanent building was never built), include six spring-fed carp ponds, gardens, and picnic areas. A reproduction of a domed, branch-constructed hut honors Miwok tribal history and a newly constructed chapel on the mission site commemorates its founding.

Above: From many vantage points in the Sonoma Valley, the nearby foothills offer a breath-taking landscape as well as grazing land for cattle, sheep, and horses.

Left and following pages: The Sonoma Valley is planted to vineyards that become tourist attractions in and of themselves, colorful with seasonal changes. From August through September into October, the exciting "crush" time fills the valley's air with aromas of chocolate or vinegar. Today, the Céja family carries on the Mexican heritage of grape growing on land once used by General Vallejo. Winemaker Sal Godinez is also part of this Hispanic tradition.

Above: Displayed at the museum at Jack London State Park is a reproduction of London's study, created entirely with furnishings used by the author. London, who owned a ranch in Glen Ellen, wrote about the area in The Valley of the Moon. *From his study he also wrote many of the other books, short stories, and articles that made him famous. The ship's bell, chronometer, and barometer are from the* Shark, *the ship in which London and his wife Charmian cruised the South Pacific.*

room's chateau architecture, formal rose gardens, and picnic grounds. Throughout Sonoma County, gourmet restaurants are widely renowned for their fresh, innovative California cuisine.

One of the most recent and exciting of Sonoma's offerings, destined to grow into a full-fledged industry, is olive oil. Beginning with the first trees planted by the Russians at Fort Ross in 1812 and trees later brought by the Franciscan fathers, Sonoma now boasts 41 of the 389 registered olive oil companies in California. If the winery business is any indication, the future holds more than the annual Olive Festival as an attraction. Tasting rooms and tours are creeping into visibility, as businesses such as L'Olivier and Chalk Hill Clematis, and wineries such as Viansa, Gloria Ferrer, B.R. Cohn, Iron Horse, and Barbitta & Benziger offer their own brands of the golden oil. On the brink of an explosion, the olive oil craze is infiltrating the beauty and bath industry, as well.

Sonoma features a stunning natural environment, a rich history, superb examples of diverse architectural styles, and a robust economy fueled by production of the finest agricultural products—assets whose sum creates vast opportunity. With all that they have going for them, the residents of Sonoma could be bedeviled by all of the deadly sins. And yet they are generous, friendly, unpretentious, and welcoming. The community members— notably those who live in the twenty residences featured in this book—are the final and perhaps most important piece in the puzzle that makes Sonoma such a magical place.

CASTEÑADA ADOBE

Previous pages: The historic Casteñada Adobe is one of the oldest residences in California and is believed to have been built by Captain Don Salvador Vallejo, General Vallejo's brother. The house's simple single-story plan that gives the front facade a serene appearance is a typical vernacular Spanish design.

Left: The private manicured garden uses a mix of English and Mediterranean themes that use a predominately white and green color scheme. Its brick pathways connect a parterred herb garden, groupings of Iceberg roses, a linear arrangement of lavender de Provence, and a seating area canopied with a wisteria-laden trellis with a Mexican-style fountain nearby.

Below: The master bedroom's doors open onto an intimate outdoor sunning area, where a carved antique marble fountainhead from Spain is set into a protective stucco wall and an English lead planter has been transformed into the fountain's base. Teak benches welcome lounging.

A feeling of calmness and serenity pervades Casteñada Adobe, one of Sonoma County's few extant original adobes, and now the home of Robert and Leslie Demler. As the stillness envelops you there is no denying the solidity and significance of the structure. As early as 1837, during the Mexican period of California's history, it is believed that Captain Don Salvador Vallejo, General Vallejo's brother, began construction of this residence near Sonoma Plaza. The general's private secretary, Don Juan Casteñada, is believed to have been one of its earliest inhabitants. The adobe was among only a few permanent buildings

clustered around the Sonoma Plaza. Other important structures found nearby included General Vallejo's impressive residence Casa Grande (since destroyed), Captain Vallejo's residence, the Sonoma Barracks, and Mission San Francisco de Solano.

Gregory and Harriet Jones, who purchased the property in 1948, performed an extensive restoration, revealing the adobe walls by removing clapboard siding on the exterior and layers of wallpaper from the interior. A modern ceiling was also removed. From her estate, as Harriet had instructed, the house was sold to her friends the Demlers, whom she knew loved it as much as she did. They bought the house in 1997. Jones's trust is honored by their enthusiastic preservation of this California treasure. Robert, a retired international banker, is now a financial sector advisor to foreign governments for the U.S. Department of the Treasury. He and Leslie, an astute antiquarian and former antiques dealer, have chosen an adventurous life of travel and temporary residence abroad, finding themselves in such far-flung locales as Pretoria, Sarajevo, and London. At each destination the Demlers search for unusual decorative pieces that they then carry back or ship to their home in Sonoma, and which continue to enhance the beauty and comfort of this fine adobe home.

The historic house exudes authenticity, from the characteristic thick adobe walls

Previous pages: In the living room, creamy white walls tinted slightly with a rose tone serve as a backdrop for the exquisite collection of furnishings that the Demlers have acquired while traveling abroad. An eighteenth-century French marriage armoire anchors one side of the room, while an unusual pair of early Dutch Delftware ginger jars and antique Imari porcelain complement the Queen Anne-period English lacquered dresser base at the other side. On a wall shared by the living and dining areas, a seventeenth-century Swedish brass wall sconce with its secondary over-reflector in a typical Scandinavian motif is an exceptional piece. Antique Bosnian kilims are scattered throughout the home.

Right: In the dining room, an unusual, early-nineteenth-century Austrian bronze chandelier hangs above the seventeenth-century English oak dining table, set with English Cromwellean chairs. The ornate centerpiece is a gold- and silver-plated tinware-covered punch-bowl designed by Mr. Demler and fabricated by the Bosnian artisan family Asotić. Reflected in the mirror is an eighteenth-century Welsh dresser of country design in which is displayed a collection of very early Imari plates.

and deep window and door reveals to the aged wood beams in the ceiling. This vernacular Spanish style is much emulated today, especially in the western United States, and has spawned such varied architectural forms as Spanish Revival, Spanish Colonial Revival, and Pueblo. Even still, there is nothing like the real thing.

The original surfacing on the walls was made with a mixture of whitewash and ox blood, according to architectural historian James Beauchamp Alexander. That look is simulated by an off-white color of paint that reveals rose or peach undertones, depending on the room's light, constantly changing throughout the day. The walls' neutral palette is an appropriate backdrop, especially when candlelit, for the home's glorious furnishings. A spectacular collection of sixteenth- through nineteenth-century furnishings and art fits seamlessly together in the low-ceilinged rooms. Fine antique pieces from these diverse periods and equally diverse origins, including provenance from Italy, France, England, Bosnia, Spain, and Holland, have been accumulated through years of international travel and the Demlers' expert eye. Their pieces' shine, earthiness, and gleaming patinas are set aglow—creating an ethereal transport back in time.

Residence of Robert and Leslie Demler
Historic Adobe, c. 1837–42
Restoration, 1948

The master bedroom is furnished with a pair of late-eighteenth-century Spanish wing chairs upholstered in natural linen, a sixteenth- to seventeenth-century English oak refectory table, and an early-nineteenth-century Spanish tapestry. A nineteenth-century engraving by Ernest Laurent (French, 1859–1929) hangs to the left of the tapestry, while a contemporary pen and ink drawing, "Sarajevo," by Bosnian artist Mersad Berber hangs to the right. An antique Imari bowl and a sculpture by Mr. Demler rest on a traditional mahogany marble-topped dresser base from New Orleans.

VICTORIAN FARMHOUSE

One of the largest hay farms in Sonoma during the nineteenth century, this farm once encompassed hundreds of acres that produced the feed for all of the horses in San Francisco. It took on this prominence because of its close proximity to the loading docks at Schellville, where barges headed for the city had to travel only three miles to reach the mouth of the bay. With the advent of railroad and automobile travel, the demand for large amounts of hay dwindled. During the Depression lost fortunes led to the breakup of this farm. What remains today is four-and-a-half acres of open fields upon which the old homestead stands. It is a quiet but important statement about the way things used to be.

The picturesque home, one of Sonoma's few remaining early farmhouses, is lovingly

Above: The pool house was designed by James Beauchamp Alexander, architectural historian and architectural designer, in the style of a Palladian villa.

Right: The picturesque farmhouse is one of Sonoma's few remaining originals. Its setting in four-and-a-half acres of vineyards and open land creates a beautiful and rare rural scene.

cared for by its owner Elizabeth Coleman. She has kept the original feeling of the house yet imbued it with new life. Her fine collection of seventeenth- and eighteenth-century European antiques, especially gold gilt ecclesiastical pieces from Italy, create a deep-seated stillness and comfort that being watched over by angels affords.

She hired her friend, architectural designer James Beauchamp Alexander, to design a perfectly proportioned pool house across the lawn to accent the main house. The small Palladian villa is an image of the past remembered. When reflected in the moonlit pool, the villa's classical lines add a note of serenity to the setting. On the edge of the lawn, two whimsical Chinese kiosks, seemingly light as air, have weathered to a faded garden-green.

Coleman's experiences growing up in a German and Russian family in a little town in Siberia give her an advantage when it comes to imagination. Her Old World customs and instincts serve her well, whether she is making a floral arrangement, planning a party, or decorating her house. On her painted furnishings, chipped and peeling curves cannot be duplicated. Authenticity is obvious ... unless the piece has been surfaced by Coleman. A self-taught expert on distressing and painting wooden surfaces to simulate age, her technique is truly an art form. Her careful eye for detail and a

Left: Coleman's daughter painted a rural scene on the foyer walls where antique crystal sconces add a touch of elegance to the typical nineteenth-century California farmhouse. In the distant family room, an eighteenth-century Italian table sits below an ornately carved, gold gilt frame of the same period.

Right: A custom-made cabinet, server, and counter piece divides the kitchen from the family room. Coleman hand-surfaced the finish with layers of watercolor paint and wax to give it an antique look. The cabinet's dulled mustard hue and the warm tone of the ecclesiastical statue complement the cobalt blue on the kitchen walls and the copper collection. Olive branches from Coleman's grove bring nature into this earthy household.

Following pages: The dining area is a raised plat-form at the side of the family room. A magnificent eighteenth-century French crystal chandelier sheds candlelight on the table setting. French armchairs and Chippendale side chairs inherited from Coleman's mother add an Old World elegance to mealtimes.

tried-and-true technique bring the patina of faded age to realization. The art is in the artist, and Coleman's exquisite mood-capturing work is seen everywhere.

Not in the least pretentious, each room's design is built around antiques that make bold statements in the plain farmhouse interiors. Surprisingly, ornately carved, gilded frames and puti, ecclesiastical candlesticks converted into lamps, statuary and santos, work well together with plain modern pieces to give the rooms their distinctive look. Coleman's cherished eighteenth-century French bergères and English Chippendale chairs add glamour to the elevated dining area that is adjacent to the living room. While a generous spray of olive branches creates a festive effect during the holiday season, the unusual juxtaposition of old and new furnishings fill the simple farmhouse rooms year-round.

Residence of Elizabeth Coleman
Woodframe Farmhouse, c. 1860

CEDAR MANSION

The Cedar Mansion, once a favorite destination inn and now a comfortable family home, is a quintessential example of Victorian Italianate architecture. Regal and elegant, its circa 1876 "wedding cake" decoration, exterior details that include ornate carved wood finials, cornices, corbels, and moldings, is brought to cheery life by a coating of brilliant white paint. Gardens of colorful blossoms surround the house and, with a clear blue sky above, it is no wonder the residents chose to move from the city and "take in" country living on this two-acre estate.

The life suits them, down to the comfortable interior decor that is anything but Victorian-inspired stodgy and dark. On the contrary, the fresh interior delights and surprises with its feeling of wholeness, the result of a balance of design elements, not the least of which is the calming, neutral color palette. Each space emphasizes the home's fine architectural details such as its soaring thirteen-foot ceilings, brought out by cream-colored walls and white accents, juxtaposed with substantial furniture pieces in darker colors that anchor each room. The resultant blend is a masterful update to clean California style.

Sixteen double-hung windows fill the interior with light. The current owners kept the neutral tones formerly chosen by San Francisco interior design firm

Previous pages: The circa 1876 Cedar Mansion is one of Sonoma Valley's finest examples of Italianate architecture and one of its most striking historic homes. Painted a cheery, bright white, the house epitomizes Victorian elegance with its over-the-top detailing that seems like fantastic "wedding cake" decoration.

Left: In the library, built-in bookshelves flank a fireplace with an original mantel. Gleaming hardwood floors are found throughout the restored house.

Right: In the foyer, a graceful staircase sweeps upward from the landing balustrade that is topped with a playful finial made of an antique silver trophy. The immaculate, restored early-nineteenth-century crystal chandelier was brought from the owners' former residence. Geoffrey De Sousa of De Sousa Hughes, San Francisco, chose the nineteenth-century walnut Empire console and mirror, which set the tone for the rest of the home. Refinished original Douglas fir floors add warmth and continuity throughout.

In the dining room, ornate brass candelabras on the original mantel are positioned on either side of a contemporary painting. The dining table comfortably seats eight guests in a space that seems larger than it actually is because of the thirteen-foot-high ceiling. The opening between dining and living areas also creates a more expansive feeling.

De Sousa Hughes when the house was used as an inn. In addition to the color palette, some of the inn's furnishings and accessories remain, and are now combined with the family's own collection of fine antiques. Crystal chandeliers brought from the owners' former residence are compelling accents throughout the house. Moving into the renovated Cedar Mansion was a palpable relief for the new owners, having spent seven years restoring their previous Victorian home. Inevitably, however, some remodeling was necessary to make the house more usable for a family. Third-floor storage rooms were turned into larger spaces for the children. In the kitchen, formerly used as an office, a wall of shelves and cabinets was forfeited for more wall space. The owners also are considering the removal of a window in order to install French doors, a small but important change.

Fireplaces found throughout the house make it cozy and warm. The library and kitchen are favorite gathering spots. Each morning the first person into the kitchen makes a fire in its oversized fireplace. "Logs are always ready to go!" says the owner, now a bona fide country woman.

Victorian Italianate Mansion, c. 1876

CRAFTSMAN FARMHOUSE

One of Sonoma's most treasured historic houses is the handsome two-story Craftsman farmhouse built in a picturesque downtown location circa 1893. The restored interiors are just as lovely as the exterior—a decidedly Craftsman aesthetic revealed in the home's dark-stained wood floors and many-layered moldings. The house retains much of its original handcrafted detail and its sense of the past, though the exterior has been modified to include an enclosed veranda and a stairway.

The original builder, Frederick Duhring, Sr., proprietor of a general dry goods store on Sonoma Plaza, lived on the adjacent property. When his son married, Duhring gave him the farmhouse as a wedding gift, thereby making himself his son's neighbor. The families shared a barn and a driveway. In 1941 Marion Breckenridge, a noted sculptor whose works have been acquired by, among others, the National Cathedral in Washington, D.C., and the California Institute of Technology in Pasadena, purchased the house and moved from San Francisco to Sonoma. Later, famed Italian

Above and right: A bridge over Sonoma Creek allows entry to the grounds surrounding the restored circa 1893 farmhouse. The farmhouse's decidedly Craftsman interior wood detailing is unusual for a two-story structure. It is one of three houses built by Frederick Duhring, Sr., who owned a general dry goods store on Sonoma Plaza in the late nineteenth-century.

Following pages: The interior decor is warm, interesting, and eclectic. Miller, who owns eight Bay Area Harvest Home stores, uses pieces from the stores with antiques that evoke the home's era. Miller features a 1904 cast bronze sculpture by the home's former owner, Marion Breckenridge, on a small side table in the living room.

painter and sculptor Ettore Cadorin, Breckenridge's former teacher in Santa Barbara at the Art League, and his wife joined Breckenridge at her request. Cadorin had immigrated after World War I, as many European artisans had, seeking opportunities in America. Among many civic commissions, Cadorin worked on the Santa Barbara County Courthouse, completed in 1929. To honor Cadorin's Venetian heritage, Breckenridge named the farmhouse "La Brenta" in homage to the old farm canal that runs through low lands from the Veneto region to Venice.

After this phase of the house's history, it stood unattended for many years until the serendipitous arrival of Craig Miller, a relocated Texan with a penchant for old farmhouses and a fine appreciation of their histories. Since his purchase in 1999, Miller has painstakingly refurbished and repaired the farmhouse "reconstituting its intended relaxed atmosphere" and creating for himself and his partner, Tim Farfan, both a respite not far from the bustling plaza where they both work and an accommo-dating setting for fundraising events for select nonprofit organizations.

Miller and Farfan enjoy both their ideal home and the walk to their nearby workplaces. Miller, whose formal education is in graphics and advertising design, used his keen sense of style and entrepreneurial spirit in founding and co-owning eight

In the dining room, a built-in china cabinet serves as a room divider and scaled-up decorative piece. The comfortable country design of the table is large-scale and well proportioned for the room.

Harvest Home stores located throughout the Bay Area, including a location at the south end of Sonoma Plaza. His design sense is a blend of modern sophisticated country, primitive, and historic. Like his stores, Miller's residence is decorated with country chic flare. Farfan and Miller have also helped preserve Sonoma's history in another way—they have completely remodeled the plaza's historic Sonoma Hotel, an establishment that Farfan manages. How fortunate downtown Sonoma is to have Miller and Farfan as preservation advocates with high style and keepers of the flame of Sonoma's valuable past.

Residence of Craig Miller and Tim Farfan
Craftsman Farmhouse, c. 1893

"We weren't even in the market for a house," explains Tom Thornley, thirty-year veteran builder and preservation advocate in the Napa and Sonoma valleys, "but when friends told us there was a house for sale on our favorite block, we had to look. This is the 'businessman's block' that housed most of the late-nineteenth- and early-twentieth-century proprietors whose stores were on the nearby plaza." The next day, their realtor showed Thornley and Nelson a ramshackle early-twentieth-century bungalow. Thornley's expert eye honed in on the "great bones" of the place and Nelson, an interior designer whose clientele includes many high-profile wine country figures, immediately recognized the house's potential. They bought it on the spot.

To most of their friends, the house, buried beneath a mountain of overgrown landscaping, was beyond salvageable. Thornley and Nelson, however, visionaries

with professional acumen and a strong appreciation for Sonoma history, knew that only about half of the house needed to be gutted and reconstructed. The other half could be restored. It was inevitable that they should choose such a project when it presented itself. Thornley's experience in quality commercial construction and his involvement in architectural preservation reaches back to the 1980s when he served as chairman of both Napa County Landmarks and the Cultural Heritage Commission. His vision and commitment led to the eventual refurbishing of the Napa Opera House. Nelson, an interior designer in Sonoma for twenty-five years, grew up amid the theatricality of Hollywood. Her designs emphasize comfort yet are infused with the drama of a stage set. Her special touch produces a harmony of color in surfaces, furnishings, accessories, and ornamental details that is convivial and relaxed. Nelson's use of earth tones is well suited to rendering the

Previous pages: Thomas Thornley and Robin Nelson have completely restored a California Bungalow from the early 1900s. Klinker bricks that Thornley acquired from a multitude of sources create authentic accent elements on the exterior, such as the entry arbor, the perimeter walls, and the backyard barbecue.

Above left: Interior designer Robin Nelson has successfully blended contemporary furnishings with the strong Craftsman detailing of heavy wood moldings found around the ceiling, doors, and windows. Her clean aesthetic reveals the home's idealized nature.

Right: In the foyer, large decorative items such as urns and paintings leave breathing space for the visitor. Nelson's choice of warm accent tones in the floral arrangement and the rugs and painting complement the solid wood detailing.

Previous pages: Typical of California Craftsman bungalows, the use of wood paneling and built-in furniture shows a connection to nature through natural materials—pride in handcraftsmanship is evident. The fireplace with its natural stone surround also emphasizes the importance of creating a warm, inviting home that exudes humanity.

Right: Nelson's simple but elegant arrangements and vignettes often use colorful fruit and vegetables in unexpected ways. The porch is a comfortable gathering spot in the evening for sipping fine wine and chatting with neighbors who stroll by.

Below: The stove and oven in the Thornley-Nelson kitchen is a prized inheritance from Robin's grandmother. The antique piece makes a bold nostalgic statement.

original period atmosphere of this historic home.

For the next eight months, Thornley researched the California Craftsman bungalow style with a passion, and Nelson was thoroughly "hands-on," mixing colors and painting and staining walls, architectural ornamentation, and built-in furniture surfaces. The duo is a perfect match for the Arts and Crafts building, designed in 1911 by original owner Lizzie Lutgens's brother-in-law Adolph Lutgens, a Sonoma architect.

This remarkable California Craftsman bungalow restoration and reconstruction uses natural materials and authentic period details that make the house a gem. Although the entry and living room are original, the fireplace has been rebuilt, flooring has been refinished, and most of the seven-piece redwood molding has been reproduced to match original sections milled just blocks from the house from wood transported from the Mayacamus Mountains. The entire structure was rewired and replastered, and a new kitchen, back patio, and front fence were added. The house is now a showplace. Thornley and Nelson, proud of their accomplishment and the history and tradition that the house embodies, are happy to share it with friends and visitors.

Residence of Thomas Thornley and Robin Nelson
California Craftsman Bungalow, c. 1911
Adolph Lutgens, Architect

When a couple from the city first entertained the idea of purchasing a retreat in the countryside north of San Francisco, they had in mind a simple house on a small parcel of land. But when their realtor showed them a hillside property in Sonoma Valley that had been part of the famous 3,000-acre Sobre Vista Ranch, once owned by the wealthy San Francisco art patron and society dame Alma Spreckels, they fell in love with it. They were immediately captivated by "the beauty and breadth of the land." What came next was the realization of how much work it would take. Still, their sense of wonder took over and they found themselves owners of a forty-five-acre working farm with eight acres planted to vineyards.

They couldn't be more delighted with their purchase. The wife felt immediately at home on the expanses of land, having grown up on a 300-acre horse ranch in New Mexico; the husband, who grew up on the East Coast, appreciates his property's history and is happily evolving into a gentleman farmer, with producing vineyards and olive trees.

Sobre Vista Ranch was part of the original 66,000-acre Rancho Petaluma, given to Mariano Guadalupe Vallejo by the Mexican government as payment for establishing a new military outpost at Sonoma and managing the colonization of the area.

Previous pages: In the cheery living room, comfortable furniture and a warm fire encourage gatherings. Fresh air throughout the breezy home and abundant light from its many windows add to the home's welcoming atmosphere. Needlepoint pillows featuring hot air balloons celebrate a passion of the homeowner's father, a world-class hot air balloonist.

Left: A 3,000-bottle wine cellar and tasting room is a new addition to an existing building south of the main house. Sonomans enjoy their collections of fine wine, displaying them in state-of-the-art cellars. Here, temperatures are carefully maintained to protect the cherished vintages.

Right: Among towering gigantic California redwoods, a dining patio easily becomes a dance floor when desired. The homeowners generously share their estate with worthy nonprofit causes that they champion, hosting events that accommodate small or large crowds.

After 1850, as Rancho Petaluma was subdivided, acreage in the Sonoma Valley portion of it, known as Sobre Vista, passed through various hands until it was purchased by Alma Spreckels in 1934. She restored the main house, which was subsequently destroyed by a fire, and created a magnificent 3,000-acre working ranch in ultimately futile hopes that her troubled son Adolph would take an interest in ranching. During her ownership, the ranch was the center of social life in the valley due to her extravagant and legendary entertaining. Later, the ranch was used during World War II as a relaxation center for the military, before it was sold and broken into smaller parcels.

Today the forty-five-acre Sobre Vista Farm is a horticultural feast for the eyes. The current house is set among towering redwoods, where, as the current owners say, "The bounty of the land is amazing."

Previous farming enterprises have left their legacy. The property is lush with oak, chestnut, pecan, walnut, and olive trees, orchards of Meyer lemons, oranges, and peaches, productive gardens of pumpkin, squash, and numerous other vegetables, as well as abundant hydrangeas, giant rhododendrons, and a formal rose garden. Eight acres of vineyards serve as a backdrop, and outbuildings include a new 3,000-bottle wine cellar and tasting room, a warehouse-turned-conference-room, guest house, pool house, and the farm manager's residence. The farm also includes animals. Two pygmy goats were a birthday present for the wife. And chickens and quail live happily together, providing a multitude of eggs for a multitude of omelettes—farm fresh.

*Former Hunting Cabin of Alma Spreckels'
  Sobre Vista Ranch
Historic Ranch House Cottage, c. 1920–34*

GRANARY AND COW BARN

Previous pages: The stick-built barn that artist Ira Yeager uses as one of his studios is located among redwoods above the Sonoma Valley proper. Its size, location, and setting afford him the privacy he requires to create the large-scale paintings that are in the collections of, among others, Joe Montana and Robert Redford.

Left: In the barn's main room, large-scale antiques create an Old World ambiance. The metal spiral stairway from France was one from which Maurice Chevalier sang, the goat cart gift from Yeager's friend and fellow Francophile Lillian Williams, and the mirror, dresser, and table, pieces from his vast collection of eighteenth-century antiques. The painting is one in his series of "Les Depardues," featuring scenes from French country life.

Master artist Ira Yeager gathers inspiration from his environment. For years, while living in France, Italy, Greece, and England, he chose to live in settings of great ambience in order to tap into the essence of another period or setting. Now he lives and works in the Napa and Sonoma valleys. In the studios where he paints and sculpts, he gives life to imaginary personalities, populating large-scale paintings with characters—fantastical, human, and animal—that capture the spirit of eighteenth-century rural country life.

Yeager's latest pied-à-terre is a stick-built barn—with raw wood walls, open-beam ceilings, and sliding "stable stall" doors—which he imagines as a hunting lodge. Neither lonesome nor lofty, it rests amidst cool towering redwoods on the side of a forested hill north of the Sonoma Valley proper. Yeager's native Washington State has instilled in him a love for beautiful, bountiful, deep green nature, and, his beloved Provence, a yearning for bucolic scenery. Here he has both. The prolific artist continually sorts and arranges his collections of rarified eighteenth- and nineteenth-century European antiques into unconventional salon settings that inspire projects, energizing his senses and memory.

This barn, staged as a "hunting lodge," allows Yeager the solitude and silence necessary to his work. It is filled with a forlorn romance

Previous pages: One side of the main room is decorated as a hunting lodge, the onetime "home" of
an imaginary, bankrupt French baron. It is furnished with the delicacy of the French aristocracy,
incorporating fine but tarnished silver pieces, a
handsome sideboard, elegant decorative items such
as gilt-framed mirrors, and side chairs designed
in a country French tradition. A portrait of the
"gentleman pauper" hangs between the doors.

that Yeager transforms into lyrical paintings.
With his mind's eye he looks backward in
time, conjuring, for example, a portrait of the
old barn and its past inhabitants. He tells the
story of a rakish baron who, though once a
wealthy landowner and lord of an elegant
chateau, found himself penniless and outcast,
having lost his fortune in a game of whist.
After fate's cruel blow, all that remained of
his former grandeur were a few pieces of
Louis Seize furniture the baron had salvaged
and brought to a small hidden outpost built
on five acres that bordered his former estate.
This "hunting lodge" is a straightforward, lean
structure, originally built as a grain barn and
stable, which now has an interior of gentility.

His esoteric new series of oil paintings take
as their theme a bit of Bohemian esoteria—
"Les Depardues," a name which Bohemian
outcasts of the Belle Epoqué took from the
"big, blouse-y sleeves" of their costumes.
The women wore full, black trousers and men
donned tricornered hats, masks, sashes, and
boots—a throwback to an earlier romantic
era. Yeager's Bohemians are visitors to the cold
mountain hunting lodge, seeking the
abundance of wild game in the woods. In this
savage land, the lodge becomes an impromptu
restaurant—a wild boar is roasted by the ladies
present, and the destitute baron plays host,
painting portraits of them for mere pennies.

Residence of Ira Yeager
Ranch Barn
Refurbished, 2000

Left: Yeager is inspired by objects that evoke a bygone era. The open paint-box reminds him of his imagined figure, the "baron," who may have used painting to extricate his mind from unfortunate circumstances. Fine old china and a collection of beloved books on the richly carved sideboard further reveal the character of the baron.

Right: The ornate metal staircase rises to the hayloft. Away from the main room, and down a center aisle, a sliding stall door closes off a sitting room. The rustic building has a charm and personality of its own. It is another evocative setting for sparking Yeager's creativity.

Following pages: Also found in the studio are large- and small-scale portraits of imagined guests to the "hunting lodge." Yeager is creating a series of works that portray eighteenth-century rural life among Bohemian outcasts of the Belle Epoqué. Unpretentious and homey, chairs, sofa, and pillows are covered in sometimes-tattered, country-style fabrics.

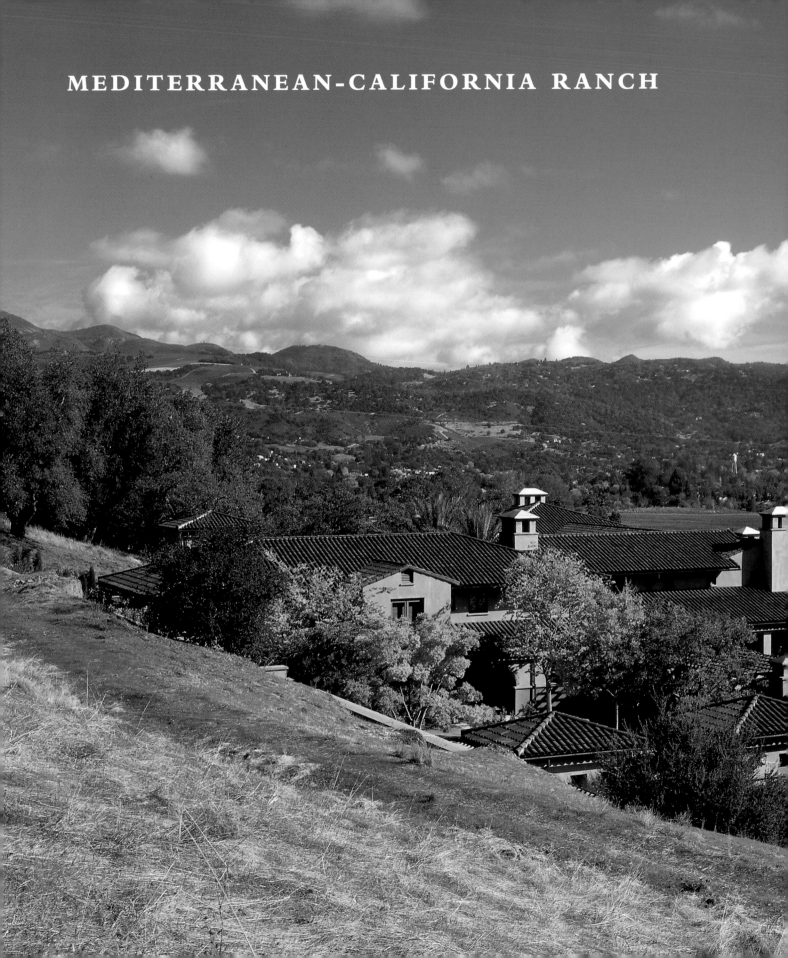

MEDITERRANEAN-CALIFORNIA RANCH

Previous pages: With the Sonoma Valley at its feet, the expansive ranch designed in a clean Mediterranean-California style fills the hillside with an array of connected structures evocative of hillside towns of the Mediterranean.

Left: The house's presence atop an ascending drive is neither foreboding nor pretentious, but is, rather, natural, sensual, and inviting. Comfortably familiar with traditional forms, architect Ned Forrest's design integrates many features associated with Italian and Spanish architecture.

Following pagers: In the family room/ library, interior designer Suzanne Tucker has separated the large space into congenial gathering spots: the seating group facing the fireplace— a cast stone version of a French Baroque original—a game table toward the far end, and a relaxation area on the balcony provide ample room for family and guests. Tucker uses many pieces of her own design, such as the lengthy upholstered sofa, the roomy arm chairs, and the central handwrought iron chandelier, to emphasize proper scale and proportion for the room's furnishings. Her accessories perfectly accent the colors and tone of the room.

This home has a decidedly restful elegance—an idyll in which to relax, let down, and inspire the farmer within. The Bay Area couple who purchased the Sonoma Valley acreage for this rambling family retreat could not have foreseen the evolution of their home's stunning beauty and their passion for the land itself. The plan to create a home with a Mediterranean spirit took a giant step forward when the owners hired Sonoma architect Ned Forrest of Forrest Architects and San Francisco-based interior designer Suzanne Tucker of Tucker & Marks. The collaboration of Forrest and Tucker, two of the Bay Area's most informed designers in Mediterranean vernacular forms, resulted in magic.

Forrest based his plan on a solid historical perspective and an understanding of the similarity of Sonoma's climate, its seasonal colorations, and its physical appearance to southern European landscapes. "Ned has an open-mindedness to collaboration and an ability to embrace new ideas," Tucker says, adding that these qualities allowed her to express important forms in architectural detailing and the scale of construction. In this home, Tucker created an atmosphere for the down-to-earth couple that conveys an undeniable sense of welcome, comfort, and livability.

Tucker's innate sense of style and appreciation of beautiful forms was nurtured

Left: The elegance of the entryway is created by a coordination of the inlaid pattern of oak and limestone in the floor and the groin-vaulted ceiling, drawing your eye along the elegant hall. Reminiscent of a nave in a European cathedral, the pendant lanterns with handblown glass add to the ethereal atmosphere. An early-eighteenth-century, carved-wood gilt mirror hangs above a gilt wood console with marble top of the same period.

Right: The spectacular early-seventeenth-century French tapestry in the high-ceilinged dining room draws the eye upward. A large Italian walnut credenza with plank top and cabinet doors framed by fluted columns on a gadrooned plinth raised on lions'-paw feet anchors the room, placed beneath the needlepoint. Architectural details of a coved niche for the early seventeenth-century walnut buffet and the clerestory window above the doorway also add visual height. Italian gilt ecclesiastical candlesticks, an antique bronze chandelier, and a bank of side windows provide pleasant lighting for the room. Michael Taylor dining chairs covered in cotton velvet and a wide, low dining table create a European ambiance and comfort for the diners. As Tucker explains, "The interiors have a European sensibility, and the mixture of periods and styles give the furnishings a collected appearance."

during her upbringing in Montecito, a locale with some of the best examples of Mediterranean architecture in the United States. This background and her formal training were deepened while she assisted John Fowler of Colfax & Fowler, the traditionalist English firm, and the late Michael Taylor of San Francisco, who promoted a casual, sophisticated, California look for interiors.

With these sensibilities, a wealth of knowledge about antiques, architecture, and the decorative arts, and a bevy of sources for unusual, high-quality pieces, Tucker personalizes her interiors with simple

elegance. She has the ability to bring a sophisticated sense of style to casual spaces, comfort to formal settings, and a balance between traditional and contemporary elements. The result is vibrancy and inner life for each room she creates. The timeless quality of her interiors is testament to her belief that good taste is always in style. For good reason this widely published arbiter of style is a significant presence in today's design world.

All involved were amazed to see how thoroughly the homebuilders embraced the land. An interest in viticulture propelled these new farmers to plant seventy acres to vineyards, a large vegetable garden, and a pumpkin patch. Each season, members of Vintage House, a senior center, and the Hanna Boys Center enjoy working together on a fund-raiser pumpkin sale. And in early autumn, artists from around the United States stay on the property, creating paintings as part of Plein Air Week. At the September sale, proceeds benefit Sonoma schools' arts education programs. This is just one example of the owners' appreciation for beauty and generosity of spirit, qualities that are reflected in their home's beautiful rural setting, its architecture, and its interior design. It couldn't have been better planned.

Mediterranean-California Ranch, 2001
Ned Forrest, Architect
Suzanne Tucker, Architectural Designer

Right: In the grand living room, a massive stone fireplace and a wall of large windows provide a comfortable formality. Warm-toned upholstered furnishings of Tucker's design and the important wooden antique pieces define the space. A pair of boldly scaled, eighteenth-century Italian tripod torchères mounted as lamps flank an ornately carved oak table of the Spanish Baroque period.

Clerestory windows designed by Tucker have a medieval quatrefoil motif. The curves reflect those of the outward curving of the iron wall sconces, and the form of the circular large-scale chandelier that Tucker designed for the space. The Italian floor lamps of wood, gesso, paint, and partially gilded are from Ed Hardy, San Francisco.

Following pages: The main house is connected to a pool house by a tile-roofed loggia, running parallel to the length of the rectangular swimming pool. Facing the view, adjacent to the front facade of the house, hefty stucco piers support a trellis that reflects the design of the loggia. A seating area close to the house features a fountain with a visually soothing shallow bowl.

TUSCAN COUNTRY HOUSE

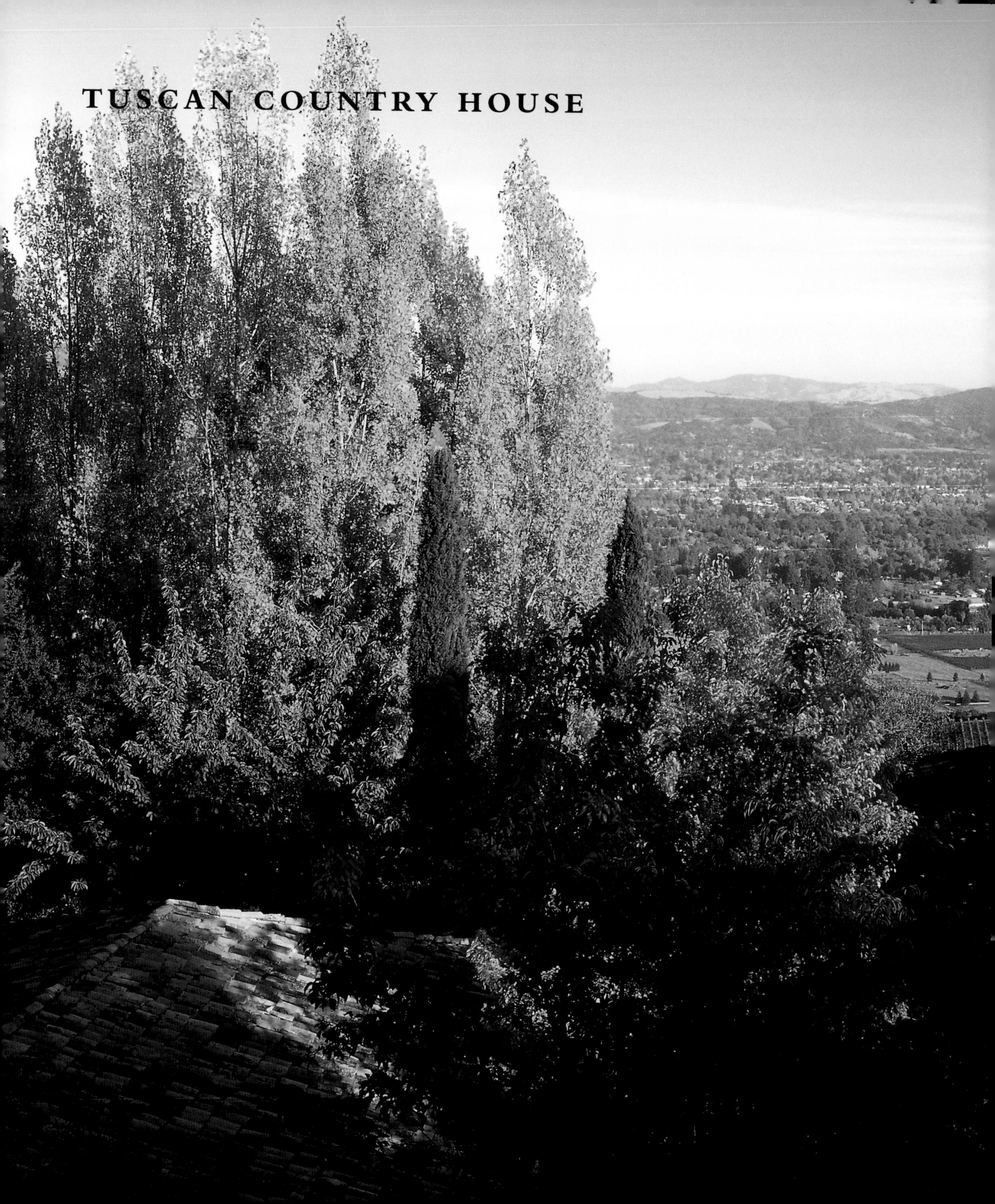

OJ and Gary Shansby began work on their rural Sonoma Valley weekend retreat with energy and an organized plan few homeowners can boast. They started with a tract of savanna covered with 100-year-old oaks that was largely overtaken by poison oak and blackberry, and inhabited by deer, fox, and coyote. On this land the Shansbys envisioned a Tuscan estate with a country house. Their ideal was realized in mellow-hued stucco and roofed with centuries-old Italian terracotta tiles. The plan for the house appears to have evolved through time, with elements that rise up or hunker down according to the variations in the hillside.

The project's wonderful balance is a result of the collaboration among San Francisco architect Sandy Walker, interior designer Suzanne Tucker, and legendary Berkeley landscape architect Mai Arbegast. The Shansbys' trust in their expertise and that of general contractor Bill Madru, of Cello and Madru, made this project an unequaled success.

Tucker's professional philosphy emphasizes attention to her clients and a hands-on approach to service. Her enjoyment of collaborating with architects, Walker among them, led to the success that created the image of an aged European abode for the Shansbys. "I'm a strong advocate for architecture and getting the bones right," Tucker says.

Previous pages: The magnificent home, reminiscent of a Tuscan country house nestled in a hillside of greenery, appears aged and solid. Imported Italian antique roof tiles, a masterful design with varying roof lines, and the massing of a family house that looks as if it evolved over time create the effect.

Right: Prominent Berkeley landscape architect Mai K. Arbegast masterfully planned and replanted the estate. Terraced patios, lawns, and gardens mirror the multileveled home's living and entertaining spaces. The estate features large foliage rather than small area plantings, with over 500 newly planted trees that include Italian cypress, colorful Japanese maples and silvery-leafed olive trees. Head gardener Mr. Shannon Howard ensures that the vast grounds are beautifully maintained.

Following pages: In the family room off the kitchen, the mantle's handhewn wooden beam and the large ceiling beams from Nevada immediately transform the space into a rustic, relaxed gathering spot. Interior designer Suzanne Tucker of Tucker & Marks, San Francisco, has chosen the ikat in warm, deep tones on the pillows, to create liveliness and give the room a feeling of intimacy. Dimmable lighting also plays an important role in the room's congenial atmosphere.

Left: The roomy country kitchen, with an adjacent open-style butler's pantry, holds the homeowners' collection of copperware and antique French confit jars, and a large, useful, center island for food prep, afternoon chats over coffee, or a country-style buffet.

Right: An early-eighteenth-century carved stone mantel from France sets a bold tone for the library, where pieces from the Shansbys' outstanding collection of Native American basketry and ceramics are coordinated with patterned, textured upholstery fabrics to infuse the room with warmth and rusticity. Two small armless chairs in Duross leather were designed by Tucker & Marks, inspired by Michael Taylor's "Tiny Tim" chair. The room's easy manner says, "Kick up your heels, have a seat, and stay awhile!"

The rustic authenticity of the house's exterior is complemented by interior use of natural materials including chiseled Italian travertine flooring. Hefty exposed wood beams, recycled from an American barn, draw the eye to the ceiling. Tucker chose to feature these forms and surfaces in a backdrop of smooth, pale ocher plaster walls to warm the large spaces. She credits her ability to make spaces feel intimate to an eye for scale and an understanding of proportion, cultivated while working closely with the well-known San Francisco interior designer the late Michael Taylor during the 1980s and 1990s.

The color scheme of the interior design is bound to the earth. With colorful accents blended with matching tones, touches of russet and rust, terra cotta, tangerine, pumpkin, and the colors found in unfinished limestone and a summer wheat field,

Tucker creates an inviting home that exudes comfort and refinement. She found antique pieces whose patina or color perfectly complemented the textures and overall presentation of the rooms. Gary Shansby's magnificent collection of Native American art and artifacts, beaded leather costumes, and rare baskets are juxtaposed with European antiques and custom upholstered pieces to make colorful and unusual statements. Known for her designs of graceful proportion and luxurious comfort, Tucker chose antiques, decorative pieces and custom furnishings that highlight the natural materials and historic references in the house. Here, an Old World ideal is perfectly matched with a New-World lifestyle.

Residence of OJ and Gary Shansby
Mediterranean Country House, 1997
Sandy Walker, Architect
Suzanne Tucker, Architectural Designer

Previous pages: In the Shansbys' dining room, the large scale of the Michael Taylor-designed walnut dining table and chairs and the two richly hued wood sideboards gives breadth to the space, establishing a distinctive calm.

Above: Tucker & Marks-designed sofas and plush easy side chairs in the living room invite the visitor to enjoy a blazing fire in the mammoth, seventeenth-century French limestone fireplace. Magnificent antiques include the late-seventeenth-century English oak barley twist side tables and a carved, eighteenth-century Portuguese console with a fossil stone top. Everywhere the flow of rooms is easy and large doors open to the great outdoors. "The architecture embraces you as you move from room to room," Suzanne comments, "and each time I visit the house it succeeds in taking my breath away, from the massiveness of the antique mantel brought over from Europe to the luxuriousness of the scale of the furnishings."

Right: The living room's comfortable character is an expression of the Shansbys' people-oriented lives. They enjoy entertaining regularly and freely in this spectacular Sonoma Valley site. The collaborative effort and understanding among the homeowners, architect Sandy Walker, and architectural and interior designer Suzanne Tucker, produced the fresh take on architecture and interiors that exceeded all of the wishes of the homeowners. Perfectly situated, perfectly planned and executed, it is a well-used, outstanding gem of architecture in the golden California hills.

LAS VENTANAS

In order to distance themselves from the frenetic lives they had led in Manhattan, Susan Skinner and Robert Heisterberg created Las Ventanas, a graceful Mediterranean-style residence on eighteen wooded acres in Sonoma Valley. As they prepared to trade careers in the finance industry and Wall Street for the idyllic country life that Sonoma offered, they envisioned a home that would capture the romance of the Mediterranean, yet meet their very specific modern needs. To make their vision a reality, they connected with architects Diana Marley and Sam Wells of Marley + Wells Architects in Petaluma and contractor Mark Molofsky in Glen Ellen.

Architecture that shared elements of Spanish Revival and Mediterranean historical styles seemed appropriate for the oak studded vale. With Marley and Wells' skill and familiarity with the forms, Skinner and Heisterberg's ideas for their new home were integrated into an elegant design that is spacious yet intimate, colorful yet soothing, powerful yet light, and historic yet modern. Beautifully rendered, it contains all of the necessary elements that define the vernacular Spanish style— carefully proportioned, correctly detailed architectural elements are most important. Natural materials used here include stone and iron, thick barrel-vaulted terra-cotta roof tiles, and hefty wood beams. Deep window and door reveals, fully rounded arches in corridors and patios, flooring of

Previous pages: Las Ventanas, or The House of Many Windows, is so well designed that it is difficult to choose the most beautiful façade. The design of architects Diana Marley and Sam Well, of Marley + Wells Architects, for a Spanish-Mediterranean-style home included a linear plan that oriented the back façade's many windows toward the south. The best light streams through the windows, warming and lighting the home. The backyard landscaping features fruit trees and California native plantings, as well as potted specimen trees and decorative rocks between the mature oaks indigenous to the area.

Right: An outdoor loggia leading from the main house to the garage and guest quarters utilizes natural materials such as indigenous stone for the pier bases, solid wood for the trellis-work, and terra-cotta pavers.

The living room's outstanding architectural elements, predominately the open-beamed ceiling, the fully rounded arches over doors framed in gleaming hardwood, and the addition of decorative clerestory windows provides a sophisticated setting for the homeowners' antique and contemporary furnishings. A mantel by Sonoma Cast Stone, waxed terracotta floors, and a pair of primitive Ron Mann table lamps and torchère add an earthiness that balances the sophisticated colorful decorative handblown glass pieces and contemporary art.

unglazed terra-cotta pavers, thick stuccoed walls with smooth finishes, low-pitched roof silhouettes and dimensions reveal a solidity of form. In the Skinner-Heisterberg house, creative arrangement of space and carefully considered details are combined for functionality and beauty in this twenty-first-century hacienda.

The clients' specifications determined the home's design. "Lots of light is a must," they emphasized. Rooms were oriented at various angles to capture the best sunlight through a multitude of windows and French doors, appropriate for a house whose name means "the windows" in Spanish. Integrally dyed stuccoed walls in a toned-down ocher create a warm, light backdrop for the couple's diverse collection of antiques and art. Columns and fully rounded arches connect rooms, allowing them to become more spacious, formal and informal flow together, and the elegant becomes welcoming.

Even with the abundance of space in this Sonoma home, clever storage solutions abound. Ingenious design reflects painstaking measurement of all of the furniture pieces that were going to be used in the house, pared down from Skinner and Heisterberg's three previous homes. The result is positive: there is no wasted space. "Coupled with these efforts are attempts to keep the materials honest—and the palette warm. To us, this is more important than

Left: A wide arcade with perfectly proportioned stucco arches extends the space of the already expansive living room. Antique oriental carpets throughout the home add warmth and texture.

Right: The kitchen features a convenient center island whose treated copper countertop provides an elegant surface and whose base provides storage in the cabinet-less room. The base is painted to match the custom-glazed tiles around the warming oven and range. A Sonoma Cast Stone hood anchors the large appliance in a room where the ceiling soars and the space opens onto a casual dining area and patio in one direction, and a hallway with wet bar, leading to a formal sunken dining room in another.

adhering to a strict application of historical motifs. The house has to become a home—not a museum," explains architect Sam Wells.

The homeowners' careful and detailed planning blends perfectly with the interpretation and vision of the architects, the contractor's skills, and the fine workmanship of many talented artisans who used beautiful natural materials for this house. Summarizing their experience of the building process, the homeowners recall, "It was a joy because of all of these quality people."

Residence of Susan Skinner and Robert Heisterberg
Spanish Revival / Mediterranean Modern, 1998
Diana Marley and Sam Wells, Architects

Right: The Skinner-Heisterberg home has a magnificent entry courtyard, protected by massive wooden garden doors and iron hardware. The focal point is a Mexican fountain that spills water into a shallow pond surrounded by slate-covered low seating. The landscaping is natural, and includes citrus trees, the Mediterranean symbol of welcome.

Above: At the entrance, handcrafted ironwork includes a wall lantern and the door grille and hardware. An intricately designed bronze threshold embedded in the terra-cotta pavers welcomes guests with a flair. The warm, ocher stained stucco, massive wood beams, and cast stone door surround give the home its decidedly Mediterranean flavor.

MODERN FRENCH FARMHOUSE

Over glasses of wine with her friends Frederick Hill and Peter Gilliam, the writer M.F.K. Fisher "pointed her long elegant finger toward the nearby hills and said, 'That's where you should go,'" Hill recalls. Hill, a literary agent, and his partner Peter Gilliam, an interior designer for twenty years with John Wheatman & Associates in San Francisco, had yearned for a rural retreat where they could intermittently escape their busy careers in San Francisco. In 1989 they bought thirty-two wooded acres in Glen Ellen, in the general direction in which Fisher had pointed. "Sonoma was so seductive and still had its agricultural character," Hill reminisces. Their idea of paradise was a simple house that emphasized the luxury of space and had clearly defined areas for each of the home's functions. They sketched the design for a residence on a scrap of paper one evening after dinner. After five years, including a series of weekends spent managing the phased construction, their house, full of European country charm, is a welcomed and welcoming rural respite.

A breezeway connects two symmetrical open-air pavilions, one for the public areas and their master suite, the other for office space and guests. The simple plan became delightfully evocative of a French farmhouse in the hands of designer Gilliam, who has worked over the last decade on projects in Paris and Provence.

Graceful eight-foot French doors give both pavilions access to private gardens in the front and in the back to a pool with a lavender field on its bermed edge, a patio accented with wisteria and roses, and luscious scenery thick with oak, madrone, and manzanita groves. For the exterior, colorist Tim Caton blended paint to achieve the complex hues that recalled those used in rural France—a muted khaki for the infused stucco and periwinkle milk paint for the shutters flanking the many doors.

Decorative elements from the couple's European excursions complement the Old World scene. Stone urns flank seventeenth-century English carved wooden entry doors; an eighteenth-century French lantern hangs overhead. Iron gates and railings rust with the weather and a scattering of antique confits d'Anduze, large glazed clay jars formerly used in sixteenth-century French-chateau greenhouses, imparts age.

Rejecting the perfectly planned appearance created when all of a home's furnishings match, Gilliam believes, "Home interiors should reflect the people who live in them, their interests, who they are. In our case, it's our books and art." He prefers the juxtaposition of pieces from diverse places and eras to combat the staid "designed" look. To this end, this well-traveled gentlemen's home blends exquisite pieces whose legends are

Left: Fresh, white linens dress the bed for which Gilliam, an interior designer with John Wheatman in San Francisco, designed the brass-studded headboard. An Eames chair and ottoman and Barcelona stool provide seating. Unusual nineteenth-century English rotating book stands, with a central metal rod for stabilizing rotation, were snapped up from one of Gilliam and Hills's favorite antique dealers, Charles Gaylord. Gilliam remembers that Gaylord would say, "Oh, you can't have those," which, of course, would make you want the items desperately.

Right: Seen from the exterior foyer that separates two pavilions are prized seventeenth-century carved wood doors that were purchased in London before the house was designed. The oculus above the tall doors is a design element that is alternated with a rectangular opening above each of the pairs of eight-foot-high French doors throughout both pavilions, adding height and creating a source of light. The entrance is embellished with stone urns and terra-cotta pots during one season that are traded for bundles of tall lavender stems from the garden during another. An impressive eighteenth-century French lantern hangs above.

half of their charm, including a newly acquired Favella chair by a contemporary Spanish artist, artwork by a favorite Oaxacan painter, and rare antiques shipped home from halfway around the world. With an individualistic design sense for their home's interiors as well as its physical presence, it appears that Hill and Gilliam

have followed their belief to "build to the quality of the land" with enthusiasm and resolve.

Residence of Frederick Hill and Peter Gilliam
Modern French Farmhouse, 1994
Peter Gilliam and Frederick Hill, Architectural
* Designers*

Following pages: The back facades of the pavilions open onto an inviting swimming pool graciously landscaped with lavender de Provence. A trellis covered in climbing roses and wisteria that runs the full length of the home shelters the outdoor seating and dining areas. The view from this peaceful backyard is of the canyon, thick with madrone and oak groves, and the clear blue sky.

The projects that Suzanne Brangham completes in Sonoma are as dynamic as she is. With a sophisticated eye, a flare for rustic style, hard work, and a touch of gold in her fingertips, she has created financially viable and successful architectural gems, all with the aim of giving back to her community. Though she is an entrepreneur, she admits that her heart is really in conservation and preservation.

The culmination of Brangham's successful career of buying, remodeling, and selling houses in London and the Bay Area for years was the 1987 publication of her book, *Housewise*, which explains the process. Now she focuses on commercial projects in her hometown of Sonoma, where she had planned to retire in 1987 but is now in the midst of her ninth major construction project. The first occurred when General Vallejo's daughter's historic house became available. Brangham bought the farmhouse, refurbished and remodeled it, and opened The General's Daughter restaurant. Then she refurbished and rehabilitated a nineteenth-century farmhouse near downtown Sonoma to save it from being torn down. It now forms the nucleus of MacArthur Place, an upscale country inn, restaurant, and spa, with separate cottages built to complement the main historic structure. A few blocks away, her cooking school, Ramekins, is of rammed earth construction. Summing up

Previous pages: The house of Suzanne Brangham and Jack Lundgren was designed by entrepreneur Brangham and built of rammed earth, her material of choice for projects in Sonoma Valley. The home sits on seven hillside acres and commands a spectacular view of the town, surrounding hills, and the ocean.

Right: Brangham's use of a variety of wall heights and a voluminous wooden ceiling with hefty beams in the living room creates a dramatic effect. Her bold decor successfully blends items from different cultural styles and periods. Antique mesquite wood doors from Africa and carved wooden folk art from Mexico mix with a colorful metal sculpture of a house by contemporary artist Nick Van Krijdt and lively patterned European-sized sofa pillows.

Left: The earthiness of Brangham's interiors is enhanced by dramatic lighting at sunset, warming the tones in the animal print and tex-tured-fabric of the sofa pillows and highlighting decorative details such as the carved Mexican pieces on the coffee table and the worn wooden wheel on the mantel.

Right: An extra-long French farm table oriented on axis with the cast stone fireplace creates an air of for-mality, while simple wood chairs that surround the table return it to rusticity. The large dough bowl and the mantel's well-worn wooden wheel emphasize the rural theme and are scaled to complement the large living and dining areas.

Following pages: Brangham and Lundgren enjoy the relaxed atmos-phere of a rural setting, yet are rela-tively near Sonoma's city center and business district. In the backyard of their seven-and-a-half-acre estate, a fenced-off hillside keeps their goats from the swimming pool and enter-tainment area.

her accomplishments with her great sense of humor, Brangham states, "I who don't cook own a cooking school and two restaurants!" What a world.

Brangham's background in the fine arts and commercial design and the initiative to always challenge herself artistically led to expertise and success. As a developer, she often designs buildings herself. Her preferred construction material is rammed earth, a product in which she strongly believes and has used for her own home. She became excited because it is such an ecologically responsible system. Brangham explains, "One of the main benefits is that wood is not wasted. The plywood forms, into which the earth is compacted, are

recycled and later used on the roof. And the entire structure is energy efficient."

With contractor Steve Burlington, she designed and constructed her own rammed earth residence, which sits on seven acres and commands a spectacular view of the town and surrounding hills. The rustic interior, with its walls that look like rough peach-colored marble, lends itself well to Brangham's eclectic, warm style. She designs with bold strokes that give the dwellings drama. In the house, she included a variety of wall heights, some fourteen feet, a voluminous wooden ceiling with hefty beams, and the opening of the living room-dining room area to the kitchen-den area to create one vast living space. She

successfully blends cultural styles and periods, confessing, "I pick things up wherever I am, knowing they will work somewhere." Such pieces as antique mesquite wood doors from Mexico that have original iron hardware, kilims and rugs, antique furnishings, and architectural ornamentation from her travels are always well integrated into her designs. Authentic materials, fine designs, a spirit of conser-vation, and solid business skills make Brangham one of Sonoma's great treasures.

Residence of Suzanne Brangham and Jack Lundgren
Rammed Earth House, 1994
Suzanne Brangham, Architectural Designer

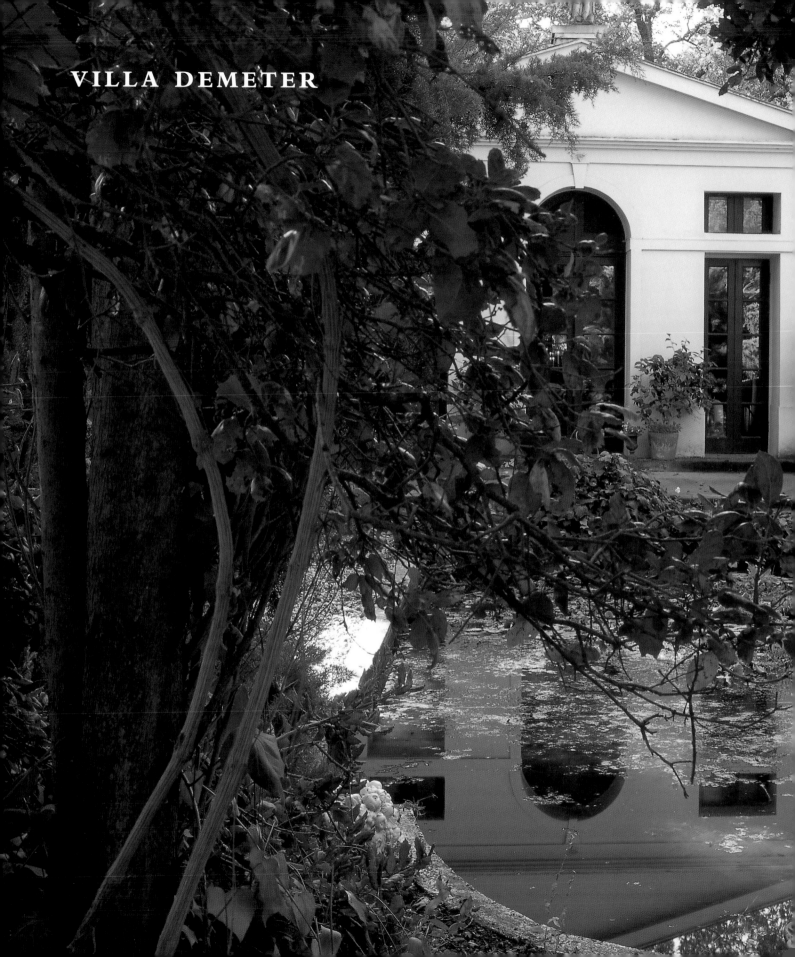

VILLA DEMETER

Previous pages: Villa Demeter is the house of architectural historian and designer James Beauchamp Alexander. His passion for the work of Italian Renaissance architect Andrea Palladio inspired him, in 1962, to build his stucco house in the form of a Palladian villa. Visitors are enchanted by its evocative style and antique architectural details. It shares its wooded setting with a reflecting pool in the front and a rose garden and Chinese pavilion at the side.

Right: One of the salons that flank the loggia is currently used as a living room. Twelve-foot-high ceilings and eight-foot-tall mirrored French doors make the room appear larger than it is. A diminutive Directoire-style cast iron and brass stove, once the possession of Empress Josephine, can warm a better part of the house with a concentrated fire. Architectural prints and original oils and watercolors adorn the walls, and the slate floor is painted a glossy black.

James Beauchamp Alexander is a gentleman and a scholar. Friendly and jovial, Beach makes acquaintances easily, and after living in Sonoma for over forty years has a bevy of friends who frequent his delightful home, Villa Demeter. One recent soiree was a packed-house party to celebrate his octogenarian status. His life is a full cup and his interest in architecture is well satisfied. He holds certificates from The Royal Academy in Copenhagen, the American School at Oxford University, École des Americains à Fontainebleau, and the National University of Mexico.

Alexander's contributions through the years have included his devotion to preservation while working for the state of California on the restoration of several major historical landmarks in Sonoma County. His knowledge of architectural history is reflected in two published volumes, *Sonoma Valley Legacy* (1986) and *San Francisco:*

Above: The enfilade, or row of rooms, that runs along the front of the house and the heavy paneled doors that oppose each other throughout give the house a sense of spaciousness. A grand piano, circular dining table, and comfortable armchairs still allow ample room to move in the loggia.

Right: A watercolor miniature by eighteenth-century French artist Fragonard sits atop a folded trictrac game table of the same period, used here as a desk. A Bouilotte, the style of lamp that was used on these gaming tables, sheds light and a crystal wine rinser is used as a vase. One of a pair of Danish-made Louis Seize side chairs, upholstered in salmon-colored cotton, has been appropriated as Alexander's desk chair.

Building the Dream City (coauthored with James Lee Heig, 2002).

Alexander discovered the Neoclassical masterpieces of Italian Renaissance architect Andrea Palladio while living in Italy in the 1950s. Study of Palladio's work became a lifelong passion for Alexander, and inspired by the works of Palladio he designed and built his own Sonoma home, a scaled-down but perfectly proportioned version of Palladian architecture. Completed in 1962, the home sits back from the road in a hidden wooded setting.

The small villa's refined facade and reflecting pool on axis with the central front French doors makes a surprisingly grand impression. Inside, a compact footprint contains a central hall, or loggia, with symmetrical smaller salons on either side. The back of the building extends this symmetry, with a centrally located kitchen and a bathroom on either side.

Alexander's design is spacious enough for one and allows flexible use for either salon, from living room, to dining room, to guest room. The eight-foot Victorian French

Left: In the loggia a Louis Seize-style chest has been covered in patterned linen. Eighteenth-century Waterford crystal decanters sit on a silver serving tray under an ornate silver-gilt mirror.

Right: The east salon's Empire chandelier and matching eighteenth-century Gustavienst console and mirror, each with the royal Vasa family crest, are visible through an opening of interior French doors.

doors, also set on axis, may be opened to allow a clear view from one end of the house to the other, or left closed for privacy. His interior decor is a charming representation of eighteenth-century French *appartement* living. His chosen few antique furnishings are exquisite and fill the home with personality. A gold gilt console and mirror came from the palace of King Gustav III of Sweden. A French game-table-turned-writing-desk and French fauteuils from the same period have also made the cut. A Directoire cast iron and brass stove once warmed the suite of Empress Josephine. There is no clutter. Alexander admirably lives by his dictum, "only buy the best, and then trade up."

Residence of James Beauchamp Alexander
Palladian Villa, 1962
James Beauchamp Alexander, Architectural Designer

ARTS AND CRAFTS MODERN HOUSE

Previous pages: Stephen and Martha Rosenblatt, owners of Sonoma Cast Stone, have created a handmade house, the fine craftsmanship of which recalls the ideals and work of the earlier Arts and Crafts movement.

Right: An open floor plan in the main living areas allows an easy flow among the different spaces. Rosenblatt's goal was to use natural and recycled materials whenever possible. A clever source of wood for the hefty ceiling beams was a cache of redwood wine casks. The floor is of apple plywood. Rosenblatt's own designs include the kitchen's oven hood and center island countertop, worked in cast stone and concrete.

Following pages: A light-filled, casual seating area adjacent to the dining room is furnished with comfortable essentials. Displayed simply, a woven wall hanging becomes a focal point and adds texture to the space.

The residence that Stephen and Martha Rosenblatt built upon their retirement in Sonoma Valley is Arts and Crafts for the twenty-first century. It embodies important ideals of the nineteenth-century Arts and Crafts movement: to live in harmony with nature and, as John Ruskin states in *The Stones of Venice*, to create architecture that "reveals its man-made origin." In the Rosenblatt house, decorative and structural elements celebrate the beauty of natural materials imprinted with the touch of man. Fine craftsmanship abounds, and details reveal creativity and enterprise. With handcrafted surfaces as pleasing as works of fine art, this house is without a single sign of pretense.

To reflect their casual lifestyle, the Rosenblatts planned their single-story, one-bedroom home's space with comfort in mind, knowing they also wanted room for family and friends to gather. The master bedroom suite is in a quiet private wing,

Below: An immense cast stone oven hood in the kitchen is stained an earthy terra cotta, backsplash tiles are glazed in subtle tones of brown and gray, and the countertop reveals its natural material's innate color. The bronze faucet also accentuates the Rosenblatts' prolific use of natural materials throughout their home.

Right: Shallow undulating steps that lead from a broad expanse of hallway to the public areas add to the peaceful feeling of the home. A wall of bookcases, handmade from salvaged wood of gigantic California wine casks, and the subtly textured flooring were crafted by Rosenblatt.

and the open floor plan of the public area feels modern and spacious. There is an easy flow among high-ceilinged spaces with sturdy wooden beams oriented toward bays of vertical windows that draw attention to a peaceful natural setting of vineyards and oaks.

The Rosenblatts wanted the house to showcase superbly crafted details designed in wood, concrete, and iron. They were also determined to use recycled materials whenever possible. Stephen secured four different sources of wood, each of which prompted imaginative projects. Apple plywood was used for the flooring throughout the house. The unusual process in which boards were cut into one-inch strips, then turned ninety degrees, and then finally laminated together created an "end grain" pattern with a subtle texture. "The repetitive nature of the design has a very calming effect," says Stephen. He then found redwood wine casks for sale in California's Central Valley that measured sixteen feet high and six feet wide. The wood from these casks became doors, bookshelves, and the larger ceiling beams. "You could smell the wine when the wood was cut," Rosenblatt recalls. He dismantled a warehouse in Oakland and used its Douglas fir for the kitchen island and that room's ceiling and beams. He also purchased a twelve-foot-tall, fifty-four-inch-diameter walnut tree that had fallen across a Sonoma bridge. Its trunk became

The spectacular twelve-foot single-slab dining room tabletop is made from the trunk of a walnut tree. A room of windows allows the visitor to appreciate the property's vineyards.

the home's dining room table and front door, each one made of a solid fifty-four-inch plank.

Rosenblatt covered his patio with pavers of his own design that reminded him of medieval cobblestones. He also had carpenter Dave Jensen fashion concrete countertops. When the residence was completed, visiting architects and designers who had come to see its environment-friendly rastra construction inquired enthusiastically about the "pillow pavers" and countertops. Rosenblatt couldn't resist, and succumbed to the failure of his retirement. In 1997 he formed Sonoma Cast Stone to sell the pavers and a line of cast stone vessel sinks, styled after English washstands. Dave Jensen joined shortly thereafter, and in 1998, when Ann Sacks decided to sell the line in her design stores and through one hundred dealers, Rosenblatt's retirement from retirement was set in (cast) stone.

Residence of Stephen and Martha Rosenblatt
Arts and Crafts Modern, 1995
Stephen and Martha Rosenblatt, Architectural
  Designers

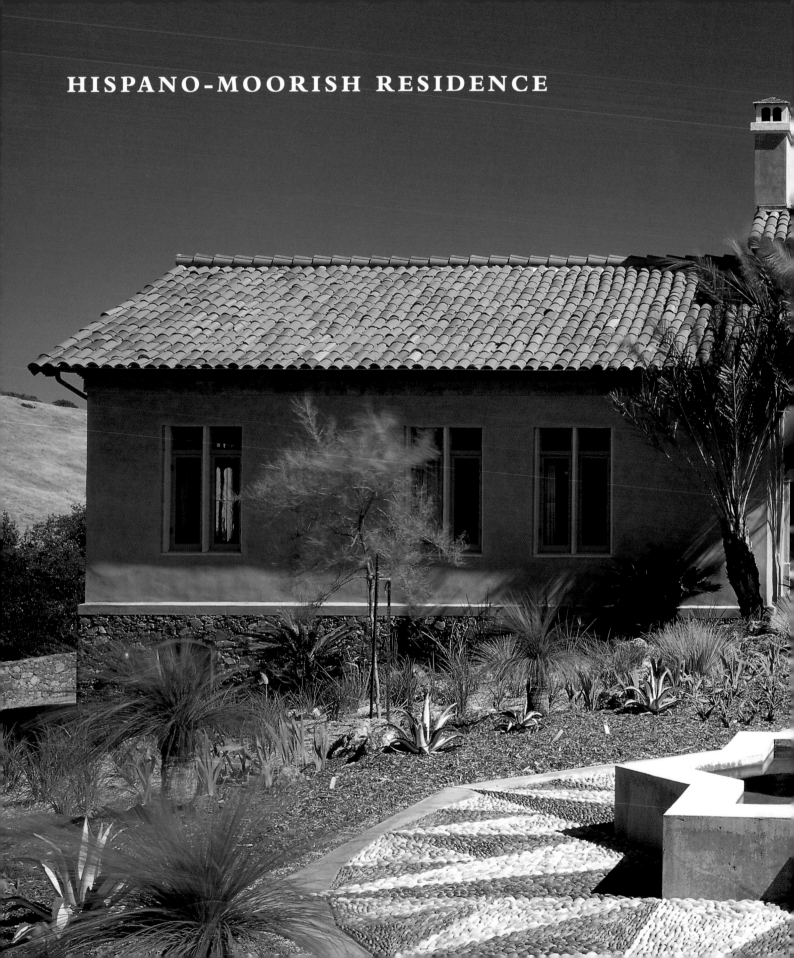

Previous pages: The house of Alber Saleh and Bart Jones sits on a ridge surrounded by vast rolling hills, recalling an image of the Alhambra, the grand Moorish palace-fort in Andalusian Spain. At the home's entrance a traditional eight-pointed-star-shaped fountain is set on axis with the front door. Mediterranean landscaping by landscape designer Brandon Tyson utilizes palms as essential parts of the romantic scheme.

Right: The living room's sensual, exotic atmosphere is created by rich deep tones in the upholstery and furnishings. French cotton is used for the draperies and sofas by George Smith from England. The highly ornamented carved wood settee, chairs, and small tables are authentic pieces from Morocco. An unusual piece that designer Brandon Tyson found for the house is a circular wooden Tibetan Thai bandstand. After much refurbishing, silvered glass was added to the top, transforming it into a glistening, whimsical coffee table that amps up the tone of the room even more. The pendant sconce, designed by Saleh, is handblown glass and iron. The coffered ceiling, fourteen feet high, is redwood and Douglas fir. Walls are plaster and molded cement.

In 1997, when partners Alber Saleh and Bart Jones first broke ground on their thirty acres of Sonoman hills and dales, they hoped that an enterprising vision and hard work would eventually turn the land into an energy efficient, sustainable, productive agrarian estate. Six years later this mortgage broker and his partner found themselves managing a grove of 600 olive trees, six acres of vineyard planted to Cabernet, and a herd of goats. And a spectacular Hispano-Moorish palace-like residence, situated on the crest of a ridge and surrounded by lush gardens and water elements, is the exquisite centerpiece.

Natural elements of the open countryside of Sonoma Valley set a European tone for the residence, painted a warm honey-yellow with shutters accented a mild bluish-green. Because the homeowners value authenticity, craftsmen transformed traditional materials into exquisite works of art that include handwrought iron filigreed grilles and gates, a colorful glazed-tile fountain, and the intricate geometric patterns of terrazzo marble flooring that luxuriously binds the kitchen with its entry patio.

Saleh and Jones's resolve to build sustainable architecture led them to Gary Black, inventor of Spar Membrane Strawbale Construction system. Strawbale construction uses concrete bond beams,

rebar grids, and sprayed-on gunite, explains Jones, who managed the construction. The residential compound, with well-scaled massing configured by architect Gary Black conjures images of the Alhambra in Granada, Spain. Saleh's innate sense of high style and his memories of the architecture and decor of his homeland, Palestine, are apparent in the expressive details of the house, which also includes elements from the Hispano-Moorish tradition and Italian rural vernacular.

Water is an important feature in traditional Spanish-Moorish architecture, as seen in the home's central open-air courtyard fountain. Also important is a design based on formal axes. Strong expressions of these elements are found in a tiled runnel that guides water from the inner courtyard fountain toward the backyard pool and patio that are open to the expansive scenery. Another fountain, which celebrates the front entrance, is set on axis with the two-story tower. It has a traditional eight-pointed-star shape, complete with a gleaming bronze lotus-shaped sculpture.

The home's sensuous, dramatic interior displays Old World elegance. Saleh explored unconventional solutions that evoed into a deeply personal style. The house became a canvas painted with rich amber and deep reds. Textured silk draperies, sofas, ottomans, and pillows create palpable luxury. Saleh's bold designs, for lighting

fixtures of blown glass and iron, and generously proportioned furniture, perfect each room's ambiance. And local artists' custom creations—such as the kitchen's hand-crafted center island of solid walnut with a Blue Azul limestone countertop, the library's coffered mahogany ceiling that has been hand stenciled in the Mudejar tradition, and a fireplace surround made of hand-hammered repoussé copper—are spectacular.

Garden designer Brandon Tyson planned for the immense landscaping program to be completed in phases, starting with the water system. His vision of a paradise that blends tropical and temperate plantings is now a series of magnificent gardens that include eight species of palms and numerous other tropical plants, enhancing the Mediterranean splendor of the house to create a truly exotic scene.

Residence of Alber Saleh and Bart Jones
Hispano-Moorish / Italian Vernacular Residence,
*   2003*
R. Gary Black, Architect
Alber Saleh, Architectural Designer

Previous pages: An exterior covered open-air patio extends the entry courtyard as well as the living space. Connected to the kitchen by large bi-folding doors, and open to the courtyard through wide arches, the area's versatility allows it to be used for receptions or casual dining. The terrazzo floors are made in the Old World style with no brass strips in between the pieces of Jerusalem limestone and Blue Azul. The over-scaled, deep-seated iron chairs are Saleh's design. The blue glazed urn is from Cozumel.

Right: A monolithic cast cement block provides fireplaces for both kitchen and adjacent library. The evocative copper fireplace surround, screened doors, and all of the home's custom ironwork was made by Gordon Kirby, considered an Old World master, at George's Forge in Sonoma. He taught himself the repoussé method in order to fulfill this commission. The intricate geometrically-patterned ceiling painting in the kitchen and library was designed and executed by artist Christina Heim of Design for Artful Living. In the kitchen, the center island's cabinets were painted to match the Blue Azul limestone countertops.

Following pages: Landscape designer Brandon Tyson's plan for the estate included a hardscape using natural materials of rock and terra cotta. A stone wall on the perimeter of the pool area separates it from a lower patio-barbecue area, the Italian cypress-flanked rose garden, and beyond, orchards and hills with oak trees. Tyson's use of exotic, tropical, and temperate plantings creates an enchanting, lush setting for the spectacular residence. Poolside, Saleh's design for a series of lounges is low and sturdy. Mattress-like cushions and bolster pillows were custom made.

To say that Stanley Abercrombie and Paul Vieyra have put a lot of thought into the design of their dream house in the eastern foothills of Sonoma is an understatement. After spending thirty-five years on the cutting edge of interior design, as Abercrombie and Vieyra have, if they didn't know what they wanted, at least they knew the choices. The walls of bookshelves that reach to eleven-foot ceilings and hold a collection of nine thousand volumes on architecture, interior design, and the decorative arts attest to this. Here, these veteran professionals created a knockout modernist house, comfortable and finely appointed, that suits them perfectly.

Both gentlemen have had distinguished careers in the design field. Abercrombie, a fellow of the American Institute of Architects, is a former editor-in-chief of *Interiors* magazine, a former editorial director and vice president of *Interior Design* magazine, and a former senior editor of architecture for the *AIA Journal*. He is also the author of numerous books on design, the latest of which is *A Century of Design 1900-2000*. Vieyra, a former senior designer for the legendary architectural firm Skidmore Owings and Merrill, was also a senior designer in the New York offices of Gensler, one of the largest architectural and design firms in the world.

During a speaking engagement at the San Francisco Design Center in the

Previous pages:
The house of Stanley Abercrombie and Paul Vieyra is constructed of rastra block, which utilizes earth inside and out. Built on a hillside, the house's rear facade contains immense sliding glass doors that provide access to the entertainment deck and the canyon immediately beyond. Completed in 1997, the modern design is sophisticated and relaxed, much like its owners.

Right: The voluminous yet intimate living room contains a sheer wall of glass that allows an expansive view of their pristine oak-laden canyon. Abercrombie has created high walls of bookcases throughout that hold his massive collection of books on architecture, interior design, and the decorative arts.

Above: Having both worked in the field of interior design for over twenty years, Abercrombie and Vieyra have developed refined taste that is easily seen in their home's modern decor. A leather sofa by Davis Allen of Skidmore Owings and Merrill is a replica of one designed for David Rockefeller for his office at Chase Manhattan Bank. Wicker chairs were designed by Marcel Breuer in 1928. The natural materials are both sleek and comfortable. An industrial quality shown in chrome accents and the fireplace surround of perforated steel panels that Vieyra designed is mitigated by the introduction of warm-toned wood in the ceiling, a rosewood screen by Charles and Ray Eames, and an antique trunk. The space is opened and enlivened by visual movement among a wall of floor-to-ceiling doors and windows that draw attention out beyond the room, a horizontality emphasized by the smooth ledge of cast concrete that becomes a seating area, and by eleven-foot-high bookcases that draw the eye upward at each end of the room.

Right: Low, wide steps of cast concrete on either side of the fireplace in the living room create a peaceful transition to the upper, main level that includes the kitchen and its adjacent dining area (pictured here), along with the private and guest wings of the house. The interior reveals the natural rough texture of eighteen-inch-thick "shot earth" walls.

mid-1980s, these Manhattanites were invited to a luncheon in the vineyards of wine country. They immediately loved the area and began a search that brought them to the Napa and Sonoma valleys many times in order to look at property. They purchased five acres in Sonoma in 1987 and did "a design a week for *years*," they say. When they moved west in 1995, they hired Jacques Mathieu, principal in Ma Terre International as construction consultant, hired structural and mechanical engineers, and built the house they had designed.

They used rastra block construction, a permanent framework system that is a great insulator and very energy efficient. The system uses grids of Thastyron, a lightweight product that is eighty-five percent recycled polystyrene. Because the grids contain hollow channels throughout, they are easily maneuvered in twelve-and-a-half-square-foot sections. After positioning the grids, concrete is poured into the channels for stabilization. Four inches of "shot earth" cover the walls inside and out, bring the thickness to eighteen inches, and produce a definitive rough texture. This rich earthiness complements other natural materials, such as the integrally dyed concrete floors, perforated steel fireplace surround, and the leather and natural-fiber fabrics that are used throughout the interior.

Left: Integrally dyed rust-toned concrete floors throughout the house create a continuum between rooms and levels. Walls made of either bookcases built flush to conserve space or textured "shot earth" and smooth wood-beamed ceilings are experienced as "surface" works of art.

Right: The foyer's literal and visual connection to the natural landscape through a large entry door and windows and lack of applied color on the walls and flooring create a low-key, settled feeling of welcome. Abercrombie and Vieyra believe that conscious placement of pieces of furniture turns them into art objects. Abercrombie has written that the two things to remember about details are that they have a character of their own and that their character should reinforce the overall impression sought in a room's design. Among abundant examples of these philosophies manifested throughout the house are a pair of upholstered laminated wood lounge chairs, designed by Marcel Breuer in 1935, that are positioned on a vegetable-dyed patterned area rug to accent the living room area just inside the entry.

Revered by the local design intelligencia and active in the Bay Area's art scene and social circles, this suave couple frequents the city to see friends and attend opera, symphony, and ballet performances. And when they entertain in Sonoma, whether inside their refined modernist home or outside on one of their private back decks that overlook an oak-laden canyon, guests always find the conversation engaging, fluid, and memorable.

Residence of Stanley Abercrombie and Paul Vieyra
Modernist House, 1997
Stanley Abercrombie, Architect
Paul Vieyra, Architectural Designer

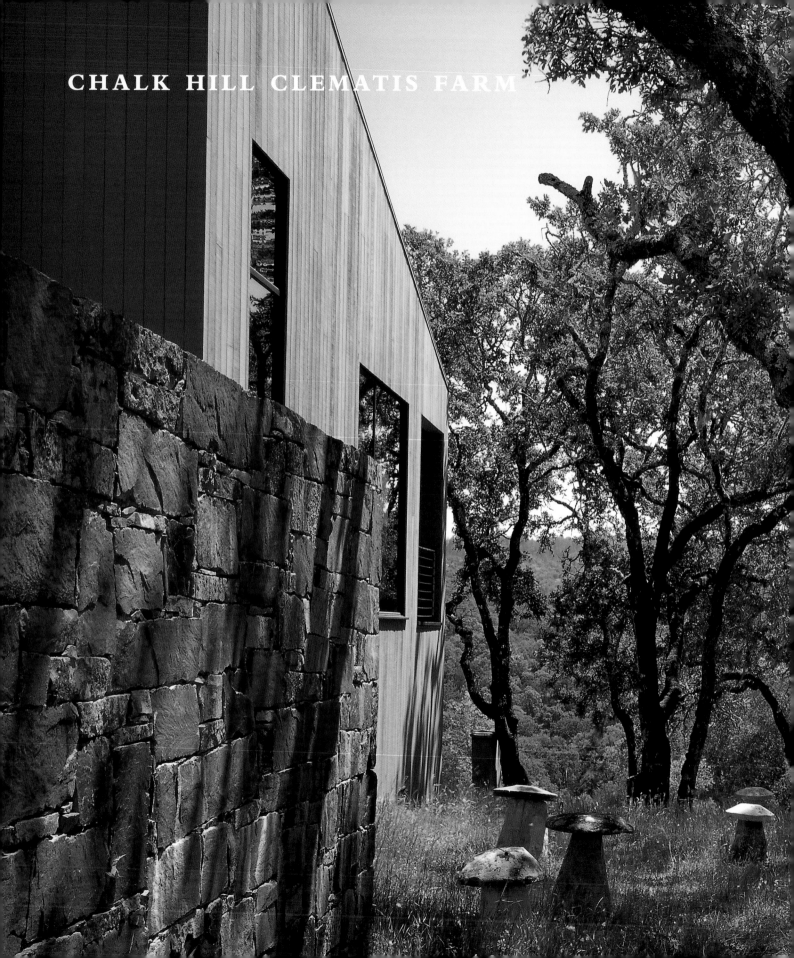

CHALK HILL CLEMATIS FARM

Previous pages: The house of Richard and Kaye Heafey sits on their 120-acre Chalk Hill Clematis Farm, where ten acres are devoted to their award-winning clematis and roses. Richard Cordello, a San Francisco-based interior designer, contributed to the extensive remodel of the ranch-style home where dry-stacked stone walls complement the natural wood siding. Early-eighteenth-century Irish staddle stones serve as landscape ornaments. Also known as mushroom stones, they once elevated barns and granaries aboveground, their saucer-like design insuring protection from grain-robbing rodents.

Left: A dramatic eighteen-foot gallery connects the Great Room to the rest of the house. Begun with one painting that served as a theme for the Heafeys' rural home, a magnificent collection of nineteenth- and twentieth-century pastoral oil paintings featuring cows now fills the gallery wall opposite the kitchen. Below the art-filled wall, a granite-topped counter serves as a convenient bar and prep area.

Right: The main bedroom whispers luxury. Interior designer Richard Cardello chose exquisite hand-embroidered Indian cotton by Jack Lenor Larsen for draperies and to cover the walls, sofa, headboard, and bed's accent pillows. An antique French leather trunk with brass fittings sits at the foot of the four-poster bed with hangings of sheer Belgian linen. An early-eighteenth-century Portuguese portrait is centered between sconces of handblown Venetian glass.

When Richard and Kaye Heafey bought 120 acres in the northern hills above Sonoma Valley, they wanted to use the land in an environmentally responsible and financially viable way. A long commute from their house in Oakland convinced them that they would enjoy spending more time on their farm. To do so, a remodel of the existing, 1981 ranch house was in order. So they divided the work into two parts: the planting of ten acres of flower gardens and the major remodel of their new house. Exuberant displays of color from thousands of thriving ornamental plants now greet visitors to their country home. Their farm, known as Chalk Hill Clematis, tucked into the hillside and covering the valley floor, is also now internationally renowned as an excellent source for clematis and rose plants, cut flowers, olive oil, and vinegar. After twenty years, the industrious couple has attained their far-reaching goals.

The Heafeys' retreat and home is a place they often share with friends, especially during parties. Parts of the architectural re-design and the comprehensive interior makeover is the work of designer Richard Cardello of Richard Cardello Interior Design in San Francisco, whom the Heafeys had met through a mutual friend, chef Paul Bertoli. The more time the Heafeys and Cardello spent reviewing and choosing from the couple's antiques collection and shopping for new art or

furnishings, the more they realized that their visions for the design were *sympatico*. The Heafeys' intuition proved right: at every turn in the three-year project, the Heafeys were pleased with Cardello's plans for architectural modifications and expertise in creating restrained sophisticated interior design.

The Heafeys' trust in Cardello was tested when he explained that certain changes needed to be made to the interior to create a greater openness. A visually constricting nonstructural beam that had bisected the kitchen ceiling was removed and the adjacent hallway opened up to an eighteen-foot ceiling. Cardello and Kaye Heafey knew at once that the hallway was the place to display her collection of English, French, Belgian, and American nineteenth- and twentieth-century pastoral oil paintings featuring cows. She admits, "It started with one and now there's a whole herd. It just seemed the right theme for a country house." Around the corner, in the Great Room that combines the living and dining areas, wide expanses of glass create a spacious feeling by allowing vistas of the surrounding oak-studded hills into the room. A wall of sliding doors now opens onto the large patio deck where the Heafeys frequently entertain guests.

Cardello's interior designs incorporate the Heafeys' fine collection of antique furnishings and decorative pieces in stone,

Cardello's contributions to the redesign of the Great Room created a relaxed atmosphere for entertaining by opening the living and dining areas and using rich Merbau wood as flooring for the entire area. Huge sliding doors connect the space with a large deck. A soaring angled ceiling of exposed beams creates volume. In the dining area, an unusual four-door eighteenth-century French armoire holds dinnerware and linens. The Cardello-designed seven-foot-diameter circular table is French limestone. The six-foot-diameter Fortuny-style light fixture features hand-painted silk fabric and cording. "Golden Celebration" roses from the Heafeys' gardens complete the table setting. In the living room, an eighteenth-century Chinese "nan mu" altar table holds antique Venetian brass goldola ornaments. Upholstered pieces include a pair of custom-designed lounge chairs in chocolate brown suede. Flanking the Rumsford fireplace are two unmatched circa 1930 Barovier Venetian-glass floor lamps, above which hangs a painting by Vietnamese artist Thànn Chu'óng.

The Heafeys' ten acres of gardens flourish with more than 200 varieties of clematis and 100 varieties of roses, of which many have won awards.

terra cotta, and wood that they have found on their international travels. His use of hand-embroidered cotton from India, sheer Belgian linen, French leather, and Fortuny silk flow seemlessly together to create a decor that is perfectly elegant yet not in the least fussy or contrived. Nature rules in both color and materials used to translate the Heafey's dedication to fine country living.

Residence of Richard and Kaye Heafey
California Ranch House, 1981
Remodeled, 2003
Miles Berger, Architect
Richard Cardello, Architectural Designer

GRACE RANCH

In a landscape of low rambling hills dotted with live oaks in the lower Sonoma Valley, this clapboard ranch compound makes a Zen-like statement and is a fresh approach to the design of a family retreat. Its clean design is the result of a consideration of diverse influences. Brooks Walker, a principal of Walker Warner Architects in San Francisco, gave a new sleekness to the vernacular American form in order to satisfy both the husband, a modernist, and the wife, a traditionalist. The home's exterior, with its simplicity of form and quality of materials, reflects the interior, where precision craftsmanship has highlighted the refined design features.

The first order of business was to integrate this structure into the physical setting and its historically agricultural context. The U-shaped farmhouse, built by Dave Warner of Redhorse Constructors, Inc., is sited so that the inner courtyard, loggias, and a pool that is set down on a lower grade, are protected from the strong winds that whip around the hills and the ocean fogs that prevail in the mornings. A three-story tower, reminiscent of a grain silo, anchors the one-story home and helps create an agrarian aura. Details such as chicken coop light monitors, which appear as small windowed cupolas on the roof, let in overhead light.

The home's voluminous interior is warmed by the use of natural materials and allusions to historic architectural detailing such as ceilings with exposed barnlike wood trusses. A gigantic cross-boarded barn door that slides on massive iron hinges opens the living room to the fresh air of the courtyard. At the main entrance a Dutch door conveys a casual country welcome. The mild, earthbound hues of the interior design by Michael Tedrick of Tedrick & Bennett, Inc., San Francisco, create a soothing atmosphere. Tedrick designed and had fabricated accent pieces such as pendant lanterns, chandeliers, and andirons of handwrought iron. These touches reinforce the country feeling, as does Tedrick's custom furniture that is both comfortable and sophisticated, complementing Walker's refined vernacular design.

Low-impact landscaping of native plantings and a luxurious lawn watered by a powerful well create an intimate, perfectly scaled setting amidst the rustic Western scenery. To complement the warm white paint of the home's exterior, structural forms such as chimneys and exposed bases are made of unfinished board form concrete. Bluestone block in a green-brown range, cut with precision to create an elegant, tight design for the entryway, also blend with the exterior color scheme and create a path of subtle but striking beauty.

The farmhouse, with guest house and other outbuildings, is a tasteful, imaginative

Previous pages: Architect Brooks Walker, principal of Walker Warner Architects in San Francisco, designed Grace Ranch as an elegant modern farmhouse set in the low hills of the Sonoma Valley. He sheltered it comfortably against the cool marine winds while asserting its presence on a spectacular sweeping lawn at its entrance. A low bluestone wall and the lines and warm white color of the main house's exterior are perfectly integrated. The wall creates another relaxed seating area in which to enjoy an evening fire and the rural atmosphere of rolling oak-dotted hills. The compound's design is delightfully bright, well built, and worthy of its setting, one of the most naturally beautiful in the Sonoma Valley.

Right: Brooks Walker anchored the one-story home, a modernist farmhouse design, with a three-story tower reminiscent of a grain silo. The tower, which contains a library and office, as well as the windowed cupolas (chicken coop light monitors) on the roof, are both evocative and functional.

Following pages: Dave Warner, principal of Redhorse Constructors, Inc., helped to create the home's Zen-like peace with precise construction of architectural details and finely crafted soothing wood surfaces. In the living room a natural-toned wood ceiling and open-beam trusses that recall barn forms give the pleasantly bright living room both added volume and intimacy. Interior designer Michael Tedrick of Tedrick & Bennett, Inc., San Francisco, has created a relaxed, sophisticated interior design that features a muted, earthbound palette and upholstered furniture that he custom designed for the space. He also designed the iron and parquet coffee table. At the far end of room, a large reading-lounging niche, or a Hawaiian hickee, allows the children to be a part of the scene. Art from John Berggruen Gallery in San Francisco completes the room.

The spacious fresh-white kitchen and dining areas are well lit with light from the chicken coop light monitors on the roof and expanse of bi-folding glass doors that open to the breakfast porch. A series of painted wood trusses bind the two rooms together into one visual space. In the hands of Brooks Walker, the choice to leave the steel bolts visible on the trusses, and placement of a stainless steel range and hood add to the unique, contemporary flavor of the traditional ranch house form. Michael Tedrick chose paper lanterns hanging from iron stems as appropriate fixtures to add a clean-lined and rustic touch. His choice of a contemporary iron chandelier that uses only candles to light the evening's dinner has started a fun, family tradition in the country house.

solution for a family compound, with zinc roofs, bluestone patios, and a muted warm white-toned exterior. All of these elements reflect the silvery leaves of the olive trees and lichen-covered trunks of the craggy oaks that guard the compound. There is magic and perfection in Walker's design, a seamless blend of historical and contemporary influences that both fits and defines the context in which it exists.

Modernist Ranch House Compound, 2003
Brooks Walker, Architect

Right: The breakfast porch that overlooks the swimming pool and courtyard is one of the family's favorite gathering spots. The architect has created an open space that is nonetheless intimate, because of its size, the rusticity of the open-beamed ceiling, and the detail of a low railing. A simple iron lantern designed by Michael Tedrick hangs from the open-beamed ceiling, while his design for a large patio table, with planks of teak for the top, is weather-hardy.

Following pages: A view from the back of the home reveals a symmetrical plan whose well-considered positioning in the topography provides shelter for the courtyard and house's covered porches. Landscape architect William Peters has planted for lushness and authenticity immediately surrounding the house, using native plantings to complement the rusticity of the various mature oak trees and native grasses on the grounds. He has relocated ancient olive trees from elsewhere on the property to the courtyard.

WRIGHTIAN MODERNIST HOUSE

Architects Amy Nielsen and Richard Schuh have worked as a team since 1984, and in 1988 they struck out on their own, leaving jobs at large San Francisco architectural firms, to reach some important life goals—to live and work in a setting that they love in Sonoma, and to feel more in control of their own destinies. Today, though they have no shortage of work, they deliberately immerse themselves in only a few choice projects a year. One of them, Stryker Sonoma Winery, won the Red Empire American Institute of Architects Honor Award. Their seven-year-old son Henry is also the beneficiary of their brave choices; he lives with parents who have made themselves more available by having an office upstairs in the house and they have instilled in him a love for calmness and natural beauty.

A large part of their new life entailed living closer to nature. Schuh explains that they wanted, "land on the edge of the wild . . . an unspoiled native California landscape that we would touch as little as possible. Permanence is an attraction to this area. We want the hours of our lives to capture this connection to the land." When it came to building their own residence, they referred to farmhouses they had studied in Italy and France, impressed by the way the farmhouses related to their terrain. They sited their house gently on the ridge of their ten-acre parcel, their trademark "light touch" on the land.

Previous pages: Husband and wife architects Richard Schuh and Amy Nielsen designed their home in the Sonoma hills to lightly touch the land, respectful of their natural hillside setting. Reluctant to disturb the grounds by grading or landscaping, they relied on some native plantings and an enclosed garden outside the dining area to complement the serene tone of the redwood structure.

Right: The main room serves as reception, living room, music room, and dining area. The warm glow of a satin patina on the modern furniture pieces and redwood paneling works together with the rawer cool-toned materials of concrete for the flooring and un-surfaced cinderblock for a fireplace and chimney.

Nielsen and Schuh's exquisite design for their home, like many of their other projects, involves expressing their concepts through engineering. They especially revere the work of Robert Maillart, a Swiss engineer whose work was ahead of its time and whose 1930s reinforced concrete bridges inspired innovation. Schuh explains that in their designs they "expose what would be coverd by superfluous layers." With this idea in mind, their house becomes a straightforward graceful statement that uses indigenous materials to confirm and enhance their vision. An abundance of glass insures that the surrounding natural environment is an ever-present element.

The influence of Frank Lloyd Wright's work is also undeniable in the residence's contemporary design. In this relatively small house, defined by well-balanced spaces and the rooms' boundaries, the interior seems voluminous. The second-floor office, partially cantilevered over the kitchen work area, opens a dialogue with the main living area below. Explaining this feature, Nielsen states, "Transparency is important. Openings are as important as solid parts." The eye is guided upward by geometric designs that create movement, the unbroken lines of structural beams, and the repeated parallelograms of diagonal clerestory windows that provide layers of the view and maximize light.

Left: A study niche for son Henry or a small home office area for the parents was cleverly carved out of space on a stair landing. The warm spot is created by combining rich redwood paneling, a desk of vertical grain Douglas fir, and an intricate iron railing designed by Nielsen and Schuh and crafted by Robert Owings. A window to the natural world below gives the tiny area the feeling of space.

Right: In the kitchen, countertops of cast concrete are practical and fittingly rustic. The cabinetry is stained a medium-light hue for distinction and a surface of lustrous glazed one-inch-square tiles creates a focal point that brightens the kitchen and helps the wall to recede, adding visual space.

Working closely with contractors and craftspeople on their projects lets them attain yet another of their goals, the ability to control the outcome of their careful designs more precisely. They are continually impressed by the high quality of workmanship of Sonoma artisans, and feel fortunate to have them available. Custom pieces such as carved doors, wrought iron railings, and inset tile work are commissioned regularly and always enhance the Nielsen-Schuh projects.

Residence of Amy Nielsen and Richard Schuh
Amy Nielsen and Richard Schuh, Architects
Wrightian Modernist, 1991

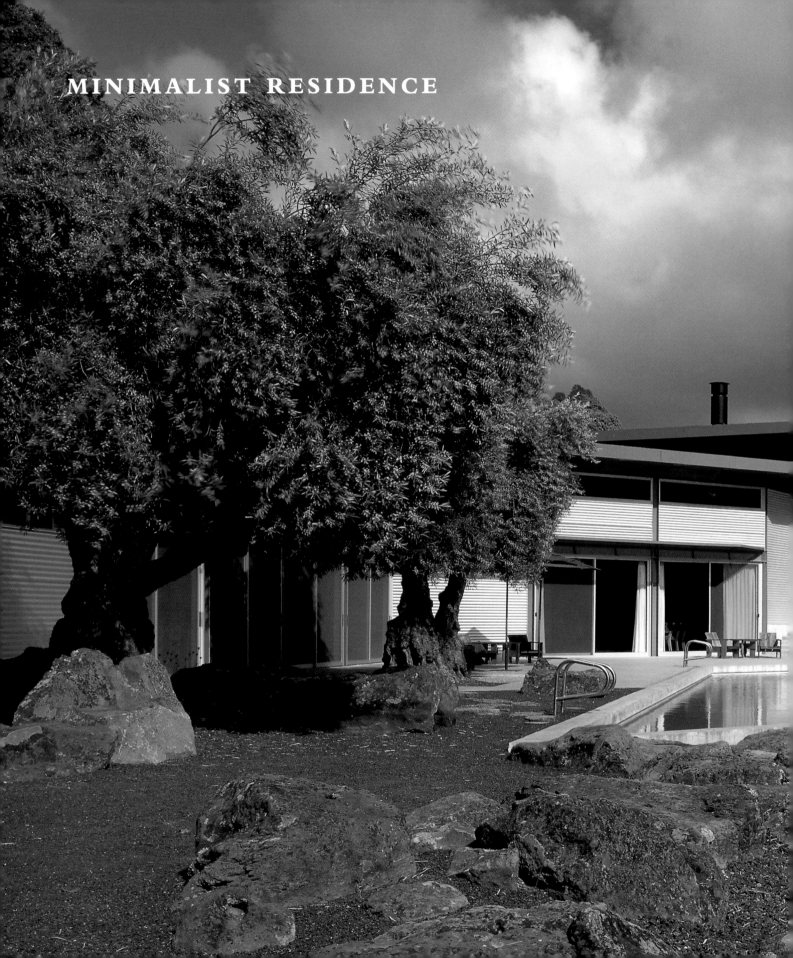

MINIMALIST RESIDENCE

The view is spectacular from atop the 400 acres of mountain bought over two decades ago by San Francisco art patron and commercial real estate investor Byron Meyer. Once homesteaded by early Sonoma settlers, the hillsides are covered with oak, madrone, and pine groves. Farther out, a portion of Santa Rosa appears as a quaint hamlet protected in a low-lying valley. And on a clear day the Pacific Ocean sparkles.

For the first decade that he owned the land, sheep and cattle grazed on the hillsides. Then, to design a residence, Meyer hired Stanley Saitowitz, a renowned modernist architect whom Meyer had met through the San Francisco Museum of Modern Art.

Saitowitz seeks creative solutions when working with unusual land contours. He let the land dictate this project, and envisioned a residence in three parts. The linked masses that form the structure, an angled presence hugging the hillside, are partially situated on a small level pad, on a promontory, and over a ravine. The bright house is oriented toward the view, with large-scale windows and doors and a

Previous pages: The home of art patron Byron Meyer was designed by Stanley Saitowitz, a professor of architecture at the University of California, Berkeley, and principal of Stanley Saitowitz Office and Natoma Architects, Inc. On the back facade huge sliding glass doors and windows provide a view over the pool area landscaped by Napa Valley-based garden designer Roger Warner with ancient olive trees and deer grass.

Above left: The house's steel, cement, and corrugated metal have been groomed into a low, sleek form that spans a small ravine and appears comfortable in the natural setting. The interconnecting structures and bridge contain public spaces as well as separate private and guest wings.

Right: The hallway that connects Meyer's private quarters to the public areas of the house may be closed off. The strong reference to a covered bridge comes from the long expanse of fenestration and the open trusses of steel in the ceiling. However, the space is transformed into a gallery by three pieces of Donald Judd furniture and a Mexican plow with razor-sharp embedded stones.

Left: A simple corridor becomes a work of sculpture in the hands of architect Stanley Saitowitz. Two divided parallel, elongated curves of cement walls create an alternative exterior walkway to the guest quarters. A door at the end of a series of corrugated metal panels swings into the veranda, giving entry into the screened-in porch/dining area facing the pool.

Right: The main living space, set below the entrance, is raised slightly above the kitchen and dining area by a few steps. Meyer commissioned the mural by Sol LeWitt that fills the seventeen-by-twelve-foot space with just-right colors and a lively motion that adds excitement to the room. Interior designer Michael Booth of Babey Moulton Jue & Booth created a nucleus of comfortable furniture, a sofa covered in linen, twin chairs covered in camel-colored wool, side tables that hold matching parchment lamps, and two English side chairs from the early 1930s. Rope chairs are by French artist Christian Astuguevieille. The rolling glass coffee table adds whimsy. A game table and chairs at the top of the spiral staircase are by Connecticut-based designer Stephen Piscuskas. Pieces from Meyer's own collection include "Dancer's Head," a three-faced mask from Mexico that sits by the fireplace, and candlesticks made from branding irons, placed on the coffee table, also from Mexico.

veranda overlooking the pool. In the main space, the living room, dining room, library, and kitchen flow easily into one another yet remain distinct. From this central space, a spiral stair coils upward to a covered, glassed-in footbridge that traverses the ravine and leads to the master suite. At the opposite end, an "unconditional space" that leads to the guest quarters may be cleverly transformed, through removable screens, into a veranda, an open and wide corridor, or an alfresco dining area.

Everywhere, steel beams painted the rusty red of madrone trees, scored concrete floors, and great expanses of glass create a feeling of power and solidity, but also lightness. Ceiling heights that rise in places to seventeen feet create the feeling of a loft space, something Meyer has liked since his early years in New York City. Walls with a pale-ocher Venetian-stucco finish and a slight and steady curve add sensuality to the rooms.

The home's chic interiors, designed by Michael Booth and his associate Sergio Mercado of Babey Moulton Jue & Booth, San Francisco, are defined by perfectly styled furnishings that create an aura of sophistication and provide comfort and visual coalescence for private relaxation spots or larger gathering areas. In addition, enticing forms and colors of Meyer's fine pieces of contemporary art, including paintings, sculpture, and photography,

Left: The kitchen that faces the open dining area is dramatic and sleek, utilizing surfaces of matte charcoal tile, glass, and steel, softened from a fully industrial look by the prevalent use of Douglas fir and the warm tone of the curved Venetian-plaster wall. A large beam with attached under-framing, painted "madrone" to match the ceiling trusses, supports the glass counter, used for dining or serving. Antique English factory lights hang in the center of the room to supplement light from a horizontal window and uplighting over the cabinets.

Right: A central cast concrete fireplace that serves both dining and living areas creates a median space. Michael Booth modified a pair of andirons made from train rails to become one double-faced andiron. A trio of ceramic vases by Betty Woodman sits on a cast concrete wall nearby while in the dining area a large oil on canvas by Frank Lobdel integrates colors featured elsewhere in the room. A custom-designed stained redwood plank dining table by Jeff Jamieson seats twelve guests at chairs by Knoll. Whimsical handblown glass dishes were acquired by Meyer in Oaxaca.

In the main bedroom, New York-based artist Christopher Wool created a piece with the flourishes of an iron grill with stamped ink on aluminum. A Frank Lloyd Wright desk is most exquisite. An aluminum-frame chair by Swiss architect Mario Botta, designer of the San Francisco Museum of Modern Art, has a black metal seat and a roll of rubber for the back. A series of framed prints by Los Angeles-based photographer Mike Kelley is of magnified dust balls (the only dust in the house). To the left of the bed is a photograph of a car (another of Meyer's passions) by John Gutmann, and on the other side, an appropriated Marlborough cowboy print by artist Richard Prince.

catapult the atmosphere into another intellectual and sensual dimension.

Meyer's vision of a retreat where he could relax with a few favorite pieces from his art collection has been realized. In his early twenties, this urbane gentleman could not have imagined that his affiliation with the arts during these formative years would lead to friendships with Vladimir Horowitz, Martha Graham, and other world-renowned performers; a writing stint with NBC; mentorships with various museum curators; and board affiliations with the Whitney Museum of American Art and the San Francisco Museum of Modern Art. Meyer's experiences have culminated in a refined ability to understand and appreciate art, and in the accumulation of an outstanding collection that has brought him pleasure through the years.

Residence of Byron Meyer
Minimalist, 2000
Stanley Saitowitz, Architect

ACKNOWLEDGMENTS

The book is dedicated to two new friends who showed me how beautiful and historically significant Sonoma is, and who made me feel at home, James Beauchamp Alexander and Suzanne Brangham, and to my husband, David Pashley.

Beach is among that rare breed of fun-loving, intelligent souls, who enjoys people and brings life to any gathering. I am honored to have become his friend and thankful for all he has taught me about his beloved Sonoma Valley. He has lived in Sonoma for forty years and is the historian par excellence of the region. His knowledge and good-natured spirit have made learning about Sonoma a pleasure.

Suzanne, from the first moment I spoke with her, has been an inspiration for me—for her dynamic personable manner, forthrightness and energy, and business acumen blended with a conservationist's conscience. She is amazingly generous and has given much to the Sonoma community, not the least of which has been the remodeling of two important historical buildings and turning them into thriving businesses, The General's Daughter restaurant and MacArthur Place Inn and Spa. She believes in Sonoma's future and steadfastly guards its past.

Gratitude for all of his love, support, and encouragement goes to my husband, David Pashley. He made the project possible.

My sincere thanks to photographer Steven Brooke, who has brought these beautiful homes and their landscapes to life. His great talent lies in his informed and intelligent vision of reality and his masterful technical skill.

Many thanks to David Morton, senior editor of architecture at Rizzoli in New York, for his continued friendship, support, time, and knowledge.

Also, many thanks to Douglas Curran for his editorial expertise, and to Abigail Sturges for the book's beautiful design.

Warm thanks go to Robert and Leslie Demler for their friendship and support.

My special thanks go to all of the homeowners I met during the scouting trips and who welcomed me into their beautiful homes. Unfortunately, because of space, all of them could not be included in the book, though I wish they could have been. Each home was exceptional. I especially thank those homeowners who graciously hosted Steven and me during the photography sessions. It was a pleasure to experience the beautiful homes, and we were continually impressed with everyone's energy, pride, and industry. It seems people really don't retire in Sonoma—they start second careers.

Thank you to the businesses and historical preservation societies who, I was glad to see, play a large part in Sonoma's well-being.

Thanks also to the wineries in Sonoma, who have made it world famous. Nicole Carter, public relations director at the gorgeous Chateau St. Jean Winery in Kenwood, has been particularly gracious and helpful. Many thanks.

Special thanks also to Louise Newquist and Shannon Kuleto in Napa Valley for their exceptional generosity of spirit, support, and enthusiasm. The book is better because of you.

Specifically, I would like to acknowledge:

Andrew Batey, Architect and Gina Martel, Rutherford

Charlene Beltramo, Gloria Ferrer Champagne Caves, Sonoma

Miles Berger, Architect, Berger Detmer Ennis, San Francisco

Beringer Blass Wine Estates, Napa and Sonoma

Michael Booth, Babey Moulton Jue & Booth, San Francisco

Miles Brooks, Miami, Florida

Karin Campion, Karin M. Campion & Associates, Residential Renovations, Sonoma

Richard Cardello, Richard Cardello Interior Design, San Francisco

John and Gloria Carswell, Snohomish, Washington

Nicole Carter, Public Relations Director, Beringer Blass Wine Estates, Napa and Sonoma

Tim Caton, Colorist, Tim Caton & Associates, Emeryville

Amelia Moràn Céja, President, Céja Vineyards, Napa and Sonoma

Chateau Sonoma, Sonoma Plaza

Chateau St. Jean Winery, Kenwood

Monty Collins, Interior Design, Seattle, Napa, San Francisco

Elane Coon, Assistant to Director of Public Relations, Chateau St. Jean Winery, Kenwood

Diana Craig, Assistant, Walker + Moody Architects, San Francisco

Marcia Cronan, Delaplane, Virginia

Carol Dodge, Museum Curator, California State Parks, Sonoma

Leslie Doud, Director, Public Relations, Walker Warner Architects, San Francisco

Field Paoli Architects, San Francisco

Ned Forrest, Forrest Architects, Sonoma

Mark Garrison, Caretaker, Grace Ranch

Patricia Gebhard, Author, Santa Barbara

Peter Gilliam, Interior Designer, John Wheatman & Associates, San Francisco

Christina Heim, Artist, Interior Designer, Design for Artful Living, Sonoma

Richard Hilkert, San Francisco

Jack London State Park, Glen Ellen

Sue Kubly, Realtor, Pacific Union Real Estate Group, Inc., San Francisco

Shannon Kuleto, Food & Wine Historian, Kuleto Estate Family Vineyards, Napa Valley

Rande Larsen, Walker + Moody Architects, San Francisco

Andrea Lazarus, Lazarus Financial, Sonoma

Carter West Lowrie, San Francisco

Robert Lunceford, Front Royal, Virginia

MacArthur Place Inn & Spa, Sonoma